Rebecca Thomas is the Head of the Employment Team at 42BR Barristers. Rebecca specialises in all areas of Employment Law, with a particular interest in discrimination law, developed during her time on the panel for the Equal Opportunities Commission. She is experienced in dealing with complex aspects of discrimination law such as indirect discrimination, maternity and equal pay.

# A Practical Guide to the Law of Pregnancy and Maternity at Work

# A Practical Guide to the Law of Pregnancy and Maternity at Work

Rebecca Thomas

Barrister

MA (Cantab)

Law Brief Publishing

Published 2024 by Law Brief Publishing, an imprint of Law Brief Publishing Ltd
30 The Parks
Minehead
Somerset
TA24 8BT

www.lawbriefpublishing.com

Paperback: 978-1-914608-98-8

*For Wesley, William and Beatrice*

# PREFACE

The employment rights of women who are pregnant or on maternity leave derive from a number of different statutory sources. The Equality Act 2010 provides protection from discrimination by way of unfavourable treatment and rights such as the right to take maternity leave and not be subjected to a detriment on the grounds of pregnancy and maternity are to be found in the Employment Rights Act 1996, and its associated regulations. In addition, employers have specific obligations towards pregnant women for example, particular obligations to undertake risk assessments of pregnant employees. Practitioners advising employers or employees need to be aware of the wide range of statutory provisions and their associated regulations. It is important to remember that it will frequently be the case that a situation in the workplace relating to pregnancy and maternity will potentially give rise to obligations and claims under a number of different provisions. For example, if an employee on maternity leave is dismissed there may be potential claims both for discrimination under the Equality Act 2010 and for automatic unfair dismissal pursuant to the Employment Rights Act 1996. This book aims to provide a practical overview of those key rights and obligations that arise when an employee is pregnant or on maternity leave including the right to take leave and maternity pay. The key concepts are examined individually but where there is a potential overlap with other claims or provisions this is highlighted. It should further be noted that, while this book touches on associated areas such as adoption and surrogacy, this work is primarily focused on pregnancy and maternity to the point of return to work and a detailed examination of issues that often arise in relation to parents in the workplace, such as flexible working, are beyond the scope of this book.

I believe the law to be correct from 1st January 2024.

*Rebecca Thomas*
*January 2024*

# CONTENTS

# CHAPTER ONE

# THE EMPLOYMENT RIGHTS ACT 1996

## Statutory Framework

Apart from the discrimination provisions of the Equality Act 2010, which are dealt with in detail in Chapter 8, the key rights and protections in relation to pregnancy and maternity derive from The Employment Rights Act 1996 ("ERA 96") including:

- Rights in relation to the right to time off and payment for ante-natal care
- Entitlement to maternity leave
- Entitlement to maternity pay
- Protection in relation to terms and conditions of employment while on maternity leave
- Protection from suffering a detriment for a reason relating to pregnancy, childbirth, maternity and maternity leave
- Protection from being dismissed on the grounds of pregnancy, childbirth, maternity and maternity leave
- Specific rights in relation to redundancy

The provisions of the ERA 96 have to be read in conjunction with the relevant associated statutes and regulations including:

- Social Security Contributions and Benefits Act 1992
- Statutory Maternity Pay Regulations 1986/1960
- Maternity and Parental Leave etc. Regulations 1999
- Management of Health and Safety at Work Regulations 1999
- Agency Workers Regulations 2010

In the following chapters we will consider those rights in more detail.

Agency Workers

In a number of parts of the ERA 96 express provision is made for the rights and obligations towards agency workers as distinct from employees (or workers). A detailed examination of more general agency worker rights is beyond the scope of this book but it is important to be aware of some of the key concepts in relation to what is meant by an agency worker and when their rights are engaged. Those key concepts are set out below and in the following chapters we consider where agency worker regulations are relevant to the pregnancy and maternity of agency workers.

Definition of Agency Worker

The definition of an agency worker is contained in the Agency Workers Regulations 2010 ("AWR 10"). Reg.3 defines an agency worker as an individual who is;

- Supplied by a temporary work agency
- Supplied to work temporarily under the supervision and direction of a hirer; and

- Has a contract with the temporary work agency which is;
    - either a contract of employment with the agency; or
    - any other contract with the agency to perform work or services personally.

An individual will not be an agency worker if the nature of the contract they have with the temporary work agency has the effect that the agency is a client or customer of a profession or business undertaking carried out by the individual. An individual will also not be an agency worker if there is a contract by which the hirer has the status of client or customer of a profession or business undertaking carried on by the individual. The definition of Agency Worker does not include those who are self-employed.

Supplied by the temporary work agency

Under Reg. 3(3) an individual will be treated as having been supplied by the temporary work agency if the agency initiates or is involved as an intermediary in the making of arrangements which lead to the individual being supplied to work temporarily for and under the direction of the hirer and the individual is supplied by an intermediary or a number of intermediaries to work temporarily for and under the supervision and direction of the hirer. An individual supplied under Reg. 3(3) shall be treated as having a contract with the temporary work agency. Reg. 3 also makes provisions that an individual will not be prevented from being an agency worker by virtue of the use of one or more intermediaries.

Temporary Work Agency

Reg. 4 defines a temporary work agency as a person engaged in the economic activity, public or private, whether or not operating for profit, and whether or not carrying out such activity in conjunction with others of;

- Supplying individuals to work temporarily for and under the supervision and direction of hirers; or
- Paying for, or receiving or forwarding payment for, the services of individuals who are supplied to work temporarily for and under the supervision and direction of hirers

Rights of Agency Workers

Reg. 5 provides that, subject to the qualifying period, which is discussed below, an agency worker is entitled to the same basic working and employment conditions as they would be entitled to for doing the same job if they had been recruited by the hirer other than using the services of a temporary work agency; and at the time the qualifying period commenced. Those relevant terms and conditions for the purposes of Reg. 5 are contained in Reg. 6 and relate to:

- Pay
- The duration of working time
- Night work
- Rest periods
- Rest breaks; and
- Annual leave

Reg. 6 further defines pay and provides that it excludes a number of matters including any payment in respect of maternity, paternity, parental bereavement or adoption leave (Reg. 6(3)(c)).

## Qualifying Period

Reg. 7 contains important limitations on when an agency worker benefits from the rights and protections conveyed under Reg. 5. Reg. 7 provides that Reg. 5 does not apply unless an agency worker has completed the qualifying period. The qualifying period is defined as working in the same role with the same hirer for 12 continuous calendar weeks, during one or more assignment.

A role will be treated as the 'same role' unless:

- The agency worker has started work in a new role with the same hirer (whether or not supplied by the same agency);
- The work or duties that make up the whole or the main part of the role are substantially different from the work or duties that made up the whole or the main part of the previous role; and
- The temporary work agency has informed the agency worker in writing of the type of work required in the new role

Any week which the agency worker works in whole or in part will count as a calendar week.

Reg. 7 contains dense provisions as to how the number of weeks an agency worker has worked is to be calculated. For the purposes of pregnancy and maternity, it is relevant to note that if an agency worker has started work on an assignment and then is unable to continue for a reason:

- Relating to pregnancy, childbirth or maternity and is at a time in a protected period; and/or

- Which is wholly for the purpose of taking time off for leave (statutory or contractual), to which the agency worker is entitled which is for ordinary, compulsory or additional maternity leave; or ordinary or additional adoption leave

the agency worker will be deemed to be working in that role with the hirer, for the original intended duration, or likely duration of the assignment, whichever is longer (Reg. 7 (6)).

Reg. 7(6) will also apply to an agency worker who is deemed to be working and whose assignment ends under maternity grounds within the meaning of s68A ERA 96 even if they are working in another role, whether for the same or different hirer during the relevant period. For discussion of s68A see Chapter 2 below.

It is important to note that the reference to protected period in the regulations is not the same as the definition of the protected period for the purposes of the Equality Act 2010. In the regulations the protected period begins at the start of pregnancy and ends at the end of 26 weeks beginning with childbirth, Reg. 7(10).

## Guidance

Guidance as to the application of the AWR 10 has been produced by the Department for Business, Energy and Industrial Strategy (BEIS). This provides explanations of the key principles and illustrative examples. Chapter 6 deals specifically with maternity.

# CHAPTER TWO

# PROTECTION OF HEALTH AND SAFETY

## Management of Health and Safety At Work Regulations

Employers, of course, have an obligation to ensure the Health and Safety of all of their employees as contained in the Management of Health and Safety at Work Regulations 1999 ("MHSWR 99"). In particular, under Reg. 3, an employer has an obligation to make a 'suitable and sufficient' assessment of the risks to the health and safety. However, the regulations in conjunction with the ERA 96, also contain specific provisions for the protection of new or expectant mothers. There are protections for both employees and agency workers.

Reg. 16 MHSWR 99 requires that, where the persons working in an undertaking include women of child-bearing age; and the work could involve a risk to a new or expectant mother, or her baby, the risk assessment required by Reg. 3(1) shall include an assessment of those risks. Reg. 16(2) provides that if the taking of action by the employer will not avoid the risk identified then the employer shall, if reasonable to do so, and it would avoid such risks, alter her working conditions or hours of work. Reg. 16A(1) contains the same obligation in respect of agency workers.

## Suspension of employees

If it is not reasonable to alter working conditions or hours of work, *or* it would not avoid the risk, then the employer shall suspend the employee from work for as long as necessary to so to avoid the risk Reg. 16(3). Part VII ERA 96 makes specific provision for suspension from work.

S66 provides that an employee is suspended from work on maternity grounds if because of a *relevant requirement* or recommendation she is suspended on the grounds she is;

- Pregnant
- Has recently given birth; or
- Is breastfeeding

Reg. 16(3) is a relevant requirement.

Reg. 16(3) is expressly subject to s67 ERA 96 which gives an employee rights to be offered alternative work. If an employer has suitable alternative work available the employee has the right to be offered if before being suspended. For the work to be suitable for the purposes of this section it must be:

- Of a kind which is both suitable in relation to her and appropriate in the circumstances; *and*
- If the terms and conditions differ from the terms and conditions for the work she normally undertakes they should must not be substantially less favourable.

Under s68 an employee who is suspended on maternity grounds is entitled to be paid unless she has been offered suitable alternative work and she has unreasonably refused to undertake that work.

Reg. 17 specifically deals with employees who are night workers. New or expectant mothers who work nights and have a certificate from a medical practitioner or midwife that shows it is necessary for her health and safety that she should not be at work for any period identified in the certificate, should be suspended by her employer. The provisions of s67 and 68 apply equally to suspensions under Reg. 17.

## Agency Workers

The Regulations in relation to agency workers differ. If it is not possible to alter the working conditions or hours of work of an agency worker, or such actions wouldn't avoid the risk, then the hirer must inform the temporary work agency who shall end the supply of the agency worker, Reg. 16A. The supply of the agency worker shall also be ended if she is a night worker and a medical practitioner or midwife supplies a certificate in the terms discussed above Reg. 17A. The ending of an assignment under Reg. 16A or 17A will be the ending of the supply of an agency worker on maternity grounds for the purposes of s68A ERA 96.

Agency workers whose supply is ended on maternity grounds within the meaning of s68A have the right to the offer of alternative work from the temporary work agency, s68B. As well as similar rights as those contained in s67, as to the suitability of work and the terms and conditions not being substantially less favourable. S68B provides that an agency worker does not have such a right where;

- She has confirmed in writing that she no longer requires the work finding service of the agency; or
- It is beyond the original intended duration, or likely duration, whichever is longer, of the original assignment

Under s68C, agency workers are entitled to be paid by the temporary work agency unless the agency has offered to propose the agency worker to a hirer which has suitable alternative work available within the meaning of s68B or, has proposed the agency worker to a hirer that has such suitable alternative work and the hirer has agreed to the supply of that agency worker *and* the worker has unreasonably refused the offer.

It is important to note that the rights under s68A -68C do not apply if an agency worker has not completed the qualifying period within the meaning of Reg 7. AWR 10 (12 weeks) or is no longer entitled to the rights contained in Reg 5 AWR 10 pursuant to Reg 8(a) or (b). For discussion of the AWR 10 and in particular the qualifying period see Chapter 1.

## Notice Requirements

Reg. 18 MHSWR 99 contains important caveats in relation to the obligations under Reg. 16 and 17 for employees.

Firstly, there is no obligation for an employer to *take* action by altering working conditions or suspending an employee under Reg. 16(2) & (3) or Reg. 17 unless the employee has notified the employer in writing that she is pregnant, has given birth in the last 6 months or is breast feeding.

Secondly, there is no obligation to *maintain* any action under Reg 16(2) & (3) or Reg 17;

- Where Reg 16(2) or (3) applies; and where, having informed her employer that she is pregnant, she has failed within a reasonable period of time after being requested, to produce a certificate from a medical practitioner or a midwife confirming that she is pregnant

- Once an employer knows that the woman is no longer a new or expectant mother

- If the employer cannot establish whether the woman remains a new or expectant mother

Reg. 18A deals with the equivalent notice requirements for agency workers.

Health and Safety Executive

The HSE have provided a guidance and a flowchart to assist employers in complying with their H&S obligations in relation to new and expectant mothers. It is worth reading the document in its entirety, but the following key points can be drawn from it;

- When you are informed that an employee or worker is a new or expectant mother conduct an individual risk assessment.
- Discuss that individual risk assessment with the new or expectant mother.
- Consult with any H&S rep or trade union representative.
- Regularly review the risk assessment.

The guidance also provides examples of the types of common risks to new and expectant mothers which include:

- Posture and Position;
    - Sitting or standing for long periods
    - Carrying heavy loads
- Working conditions;
    - Stress at work
    - Temperature
    - Noise
- Risk of physical injury;

    - Working at height
    - Working alone
    - Risk of violence
    - Vibrations

- Exposure to harmful substances

<u>Complaints to the Employment Tribunal</u>

Under S70 ERA 96, the employment tribunal has jurisdiction to hear complaints from employees that the employer has failed to offer them work under s67 or to pay them while suspended as required under s68. Under s70A the tribunal has equivalent jurisdiction to hear complaints brought by agency workers.

A claim under s70 or s70A is subject to the requirements of early conciliation and, subject to any extension under those provisions, the time limit is three months beginning with either the failure to pay, in a remuneration claim or, the first day of the suspension in a case of a failure to offer work. The three-month time limit is subject to the reasonable practicability test (s70(5)(b)/70A(5)(b).

The remedy for a failure to pay is the amount of remuneration that the Tribunal finds is due and, in a failure to offer work case, the tribunal shall award an amount of compensation it considers just and equitable having regard to:

- The infringement of the employee/ agency worker's right
- Any loss sustained by the employee/ agency worker which is attributable to the failure.

In addition to the above claims breach of obligations to ensure the health and safety of a pregnant employee might form the basis for a discrimination claim under the Equality Act (see Chapter 8) or a detriment claim (See Chapter 6).

# CHAPTER THREE

# TIME OFF FOR ANTENATAL CARE

Employees

Pregnant employees have the right to paid time off for antenatal care under Part VI of the ERA 96. The conditions for time off are set out in s55. The employee must be pregnant and have, on the advice of a registered medical practitioner, a registered midwife, or a registered nurse, made an appointment for the purposes of receiving antenatal care, s55(1). On request from her employer, she must produce a certificate from a registered medical practitioner, registered midwife, or registered nurse confirming that she is pregnant *and* an appointment card or other document showing that the appointment has been made, s55(2). It is important to note that the requirement to produce proof of pregnancy and appointment does not apply to a woman's first appointment, s55(3).

S56 sets out the arrangements for paid time off for appointments. S56(1) provides that a pregnant employee is entitled to be paid at 'the appropriate hourly rate'. When the employee works a regular number of hours each week, the appropriate hourly rate is calculated by dividing one week's pay by the normal working hours in a week. If the number of normal hours differs from week to week, then the normal working hours worked in a week is calculated by determining the average hours worked per week in the 12 previous complete weeks before the appointment, s56(3)(a). If the employee has not been employed for 12 weeks meaning that the average calculation can't be done then s56(3)(b) provides that it should be a number which fairly represents the number of normal working hours having regard to such considerations as are appropriate in the circumstances. The 'considerations' are;

- The average number of normal working hours which an employee could expect to work in a week in accordance with her contract.

- The average number of normal working hours of other employees undertaking comparable employment with the same employer

Agency Workers

The rights of agency workers to paid time off for antenatal appointments is subject to them meeting the requirements of the 12-week qualifying period contained in the Agency Workers Regulations 2010 and not having lost entitlement to the rights under Reg. 5 pursuant to Reg. 8(a) and (b), S57ZD ERA 96. For further discussion of the qualifying period and related regulations see Chapter 1.

Under s57ZA agency workers have an equivalent right to be granted time off by the temporary work agency and the hirer. The same documentary evidence requirements (save for the first appointment) as required for employees also apply. Working hours is defined under s57ZA(4) as any time when, in accordance with the terms under which the worker works temporarily for and under the supervision and direction of the hirer, the agency requires her to be at work.

S57ZB deals with remuneration for agency workers. The starting point for calculating the appropriate hourly rate is a week's pay divided by the number of normal working hours in a week by reference to the terms under which the agency worker works temporarily for and under the supervision and direction of the hirer that are in force at the time the appointment is taken. If the working hours vary then, as with the position of employees under s56, hours are calculated over a 12-week period. It should be noted that there is no equivalent provision to s56(3)(b) for circumstances where the agency worker has not been working for at least 12 weeks which is consistent with the requirement for the agency worker to have completed the qualifying period.

## Complaints to the Employment Tribunal (Employees)

The Tribunal has jurisdiction to hear complaints that an employer has *unreasonably* refused to let an employee take time off as required by s55 or has failed to pay an employee in whole or part for the time off pursuant to s56. The requirement to undertake ACAS early conciliation applies and subject to any extension of time by virtue of early conciliation the time limit for bringing a claim is three months beginning with the date of the appointment or if it was not reasonably practicable to bring it within that period within such further period as the Tribunal considers reasonable.

If a complaint is well founded the tribunal shall make a declaration to that effect. If the complaint is that the employee was unreasonably refused the time off the tribunal shall order the employer to pay the employee twice the amount she would have been entitled under s56 if they had not refused. If the complaint is that the employee was not paid for the time off taken the tribunal shall order the employer to pay the amount it finds due to her.

## Complaints to the Employment Tribunal (Agency Workers)

The employment tribunal has jurisdiction to hear complaints that the employment agency has unreasonably refused to allow the agency worker to take time off or has failed to pay her. An agency worker may also bring a complaint that the hirer has unreasonably allowed her to take the time off. As with employees the requirements of ACAS early conciliation apply and the time limit, subject to any extension, is 3 months beginning with the date of the appointment (S57ZC).

S57ZC(4) provides that where a tribunal finds a complaint is well founded it shall make a declaration. If the complaint is that the agency or the hirer unreasonably refused to allow the agency worker the time off they shall also order payment of amount twice the amount she would have been entitled to if she had not been refused the time off (S57ZC(5)). Where such an order is made the Tribunal shall apportion that payment between the agency and the hirer in such a way it considers just and equitable having regard to the extent of each respondent's responsibility for the breach. If the complaint is that the agency has not paid the agency worker the tribunal shall also order the agency to pay the amount it finds due to her.

## Detriment and Discrimination

A refusal to allow time off for antenatal appointments or to pay for the time off could also potentially give rise to a claim for detriment under s47C ERA 96 or a claim of discrimination under the Equality Act 2010. Claims under those provisions are discussed in more detail in Chapters 6 & 8 below.

## Rights to accompany to Ante-Natal Appointments

The rights described above apply only to pregnant employees/agency workers. However, by virtue of S57ZE employees who have a 'qualifying relationship' with a pregnant woman *or* her expected child have a right to time off to accompany the woman when she attends an ante-natal appointment.

'Qualifying relationship' is defined in S57ZED(7) as a person who is:

- The husband or civil partner of the pregnant woman
- A person, whether of the same or different sex as the pregnant woman, who lives with her in an enduring family relationship,

but is not a relative of the woman

- The father of the expected child
- A parent of the expected child by virtue of S42 or 43 of the Human Fertilisation and Embryology Act 2008 (HFEA 08) (circumstances where a female partner of a pregnant woman will be treated as a parent of the child).
- A potential applicant for a parental order under section 54A HFEA 08 (Surrogacy).

The rights conferred to a someone in a qualifying relationship are subject to the following limitations:

- The right to time off is limited to two occasions
- The maximum time off during those two occasions is six and a half hours
- The right only arises in respect of appointments made on the advice of a registered medical practitioner, registered midwife or registered nurse.
- The employer can request a signed declaration from the employee and if requested the employee must provide it as a condition of being entitled to the time off. The declaration must state:
    - The employee is in a qualifying relationship
    - That the purpose of the time off is to attend an ante-natal appointment
    - That the appointment has been made on the advice of one of the people mentioned above

- The date and time of the appointment

It is important to note that there is no right to be paid for this time off.

There is an equivalent provision for agency workers contained in s57ZG which require both the temporary work agency and the hirer to permit the time off if the relevant conditions are satisfied. Both the temporary work agency and the hirer are entitled to request the agency worker provides the relevant declaration.

Complaints to the Employment Tribunal

Both employees and agency workers have the right to complain to the Employment Tribunal that they have been *unreasonably* refused time of to accompany a pregnant woman to an ante-natal appointment s57ZF (employees) & s57ZH (agency workers). ACAS early conciliation applies and subject to that the claim must be presented to the Tribunal within three months of the date of the appointment.

If a complaint is successful the Tribunal must make a declaration and order a payment calculated on the basis of A x B x 2 where:

- A = the employee/workers hourly rate
- B = the number of hours they would have been entitled to be absent if they had not been unreasonably refused

If the award is made in respect of an agency worker and the Tribunal orders that the payment is to be made by the temporary work agency and the hirer then the proportion to be paid by each is to be determined by what the Tribunal considers just and equitable having regard to the extent of each respondent's responsibility for the breach.

# CHAPTER FOUR

# MATERNITY LEAVE

## Statutory Right to Maternity Leave

The right to maternity leave is contained in Part VIII of the ERA 96 and its associated regulations in the Maternity and Parental Leave etc. Regulations 1999 ("MAPLE 99"). Maternity leave is divided into 'Ordinary' and 'Additional' maternity leave. Ordinary Maternity Leave ("OML"), for those entitled, is for a period of at least 26 weeks.

## Who has the right?

Maternity leave is only available to employees (not workers).

## Qualifying conditions for maternity leave

The right to maternity leave (but not pay) is a day one right and there is no minimum period of qualifying employment. The conditions for entitlement to maternity leave are contained in Reg. 4 MAPLE 99. This provides that the employee must give notice to her employer, no later than the end of the fifteenth week before her expected week of childbirth, that:

- she is pregnant
- the expected week of childbirth; and
- the date she intends to start her maternity leave

If it was not reasonably practicable to give notice by no later than the end of the fifteenth week, the notice must be given as soon as is reasonably practicable Reg. 4(1)(a). An employer can ask the employee for a certificate either from a doctor or a midwife stating the expected week of childbirth Reg. 4(1)(b).

An employee who has given notice of when she intends to start her maternity leave can vary that date if she gives notice. The Regulations state that notice should be whichever is the earlier date of 28 days before the date varied or 28 days before the new date. However, if it is not practicable to give 28 day's notice, notice should be given as soon as is reasonably practicable Reg. 4(1A).

The earliest date that an employee can *specify* to start her maternity leave is the beginning of the eleventh week before the expected week of childbirth. An employer can require that the notice of the date (or the varied date) is given in writing Reg. 4(2).

## Employers Notice Requirement

An employer who has been given the necessary notice of maternity leave by an employee must, within 28 days, confirm in writing the start and end date of the maternity leave Reg. 7(6) & (7) MAPLE 99. It should be noted that if notice is not given by the employer and the employee does not return because she reasonably believed her maternity leave had not ended she is protected from being subjected to a detriment by her employer for that reason Reg. 1. For further discussion of detriment see Chapter 6

## When does maternity leave start?

An employee's maternity leave will start on the date she has notified her employer in accordance with the regulations unless she is absent from work wholly or partly because of pregnancy within four weeks of her expected week of childbirth, in which case it will start at that point Reg.

6(1). If her maternity leave commences due to pregnancy related absence, she is required to inform her employer as soon as reasonably practicable that she is absent wholly or partly due to her pregnancy in order to be entitled to ordinary or additional maternity leave. If maternity leave has not started on the date of childbirth then it will start the day after childbirth Reg. 6(2).

## Compulsory period of leave

An employer is not permitted to allow an employee who is entitled to ordinary maternity leave to work for two weeks starting with the day of childbirth. This period is extended to four weeks if the woman is employed in a factory or workshop, s205 Public Health Act 1936.

## Additional maternity leave

Additional maternity leave is a further period of up to 26 weeks.

## Adoption leave

Although a detailed examination of adoption law is beyond the scope of this work it should be noted that if an employee has a child via adoption or surrogacy there is also a statutory right to 52 weeks leave (26 weeks of Ordinary Adoption Leave and 26 weeks of Additional Adoption Leave) Paternity & Adoption Leave Regulations 2002 ("PALR 02"). The key points to note are:

- Only one person in a couple can take the leave
- For UK adoptions the leave can commence up to 14 days before the child starts to live with the employee Reg. 16
- For overseas adoptions leave can commence when the child

arrives in the UK or within 28 days of this date

- In the case of surrogacy leave can start the day the child is born or the day after

## Rights During Maternity Leave

S71(4) ERA 96 provides that an employee is entitled, for such purposes and to such as extent as may be prescribed, to the benefits of the terms and conditions of employment which would have applied if she had not been on ordinary maternity leave. S73 contains an equivalent provision for the period of additional maternity leave. Reg. 9 MAPLE 99 provides that an employee who takes ordinary or additional maternity leave is entitled, during that leave, to the benefit of all of the terms and conditions of employment which would have applied if she had not been absent. An employee is also bound by any obligations which arise under those terms and conditions. The only exceptions to those obligations are those contained in s71(4)(b) and 73(4)(b) ERA 96 which qualify the obligation of the employee regarding the terms and conditions to the extent they are inconsistent with the right to be absent on maternity leave.

Reg. 9(2) expressly provides that 'terms and conditions' has the meaning contained in s71(5) (ordinary maternity leave) and s73(5) (additional maternity leave) ERA 96. Those sections expressly exclude remuneration and accordingly this is excluded from Reg. 9 too. Reg. 9(3) provides further clarification as to what is meant by remuneration and states that only sums payable to an employee by way of wages or salary are to be treated as remuneration.

The effect of s71 and 73 ERA 96 and Reg. 9 is that an employee will remain entitled to all contractual benefits which are not wages. An employee on maternity leave continues to accrue holiday and retains the rights to other non-cash benefits such as subscriptions, mobile phone and company car (if they are provided for both personal and business use). The requirement for an employee to abide by their obligations under their contract may, for example prevent them obtaining other work while on maternity leave, without their employer's permission (and may affect maternity pay).

The question of benefits by way of allowances can give rise to uncertainty as to whether they are benefits which do not amount to salary and wages. One of the most common areas where this arises is in relation to car allowances. If the allowance is liable to attract liability for NI contributions an employer is likely to treat it as salary and not pay it during maternity leave, conversely in those circumstances it should then be included in the calculation for usual weekly earnings for the purpose of calculating SMP as discussed below.

The complexities in trying to ascertain what constitutes a non-cash benefit were demonstrated in *Peninsula Business Services Ltd v. Donaldson* [2016] UKEAT 0249/15 where the EAT considered the pre 2018 childcare voucher scheme which operates by way of salary sacrifice. They concluded that the vouchers did amount to remuneration within the meaning of Reg. 9 and therefore did not have to be provided during maternity leave. This view was contrary to the HMRC guidance which had been in place since 2008.

Maternity Equality Clause: Pay

S74 of EqA 10 provides express protection in relation to pay. The section applies to maternity-related pay which is defined as pay other than statutory maternity pay to which a woman is entitled and provides for modification of her terms of work for maternity-related pay if not already contained in her contract. The effect of s74 is that:

- Any pay increase which a woman receives or would have received if she had not been on maternity leave must be taken into account in calculating her maternity-related pay

- She will be entitled to any bonuses which she would have received were she not on maternity leave which relate to the period before she went on maternity leave or relate to the period of compulsory maternity leave (usually 2 weeks) or relate to the period after the protected period.

- On her return to work she will be entitled to any pay increases that she would have received had she not been on maternity leave

It should further be noted that by virtue of s76 complaints relating to contractual maternity-related pay should be brought via the maternity equality clauses and not as complaints about employment related discrimination pursuant to S39. For discussion of the employment discrimination provisions under the Equality Act see Chapter 8.

## Holiday

As noted, one of the benefits that will continue during maternity leave is the accrual of holiday. Holiday cannot be taken at the same time as maternity leave so, for example, if a woman gives birth whilst on annual leave, her leave will end and her maternity leave will commence. If a woman is taking the full year as maternity leave she may accrue a significant amount of leave which will need to be taken. Reg. 13 of the Working Time Regulations 1998 ("WTR 98") provides at Regulation 13(9) that leave may only be taken in the leave year in respect it is due and may not be replaced by a payment in lieu instead other than in circumstances that the employment is terminated. This might suggest that if woman, on return from maternity leave is unable to take her leave in the year it was accrued then she may lose it. However, applying EU case law in cases such as *Merino Goméz v Continental Industrias del Caucho SA* [2005] ICR 1040 that are authority for the fact that it is discriminatory for a woman to lose her annual leave due to maternity leave it has generally been accepted that she should be able to carry it into the following leave year and therefore, if necessary, an employer must allow an employee to carry over at least her statutory annual leave entitlement. This will include any bank holidays which are included in the statutory leave calculation. Many employers will also allow employees to carry over contractual holiday which is in excess of the minimum statutory amount. However, there is no definitive authority on the point. ACAS recommends that an employer and employee plan as early as possible as to when an employee will take her holiday and that it should be recorded in writing. They note that the parties can agree to add the holiday to the beginning or end of the maternity leave. It should be noted that the rights of an employer under Reg. 15(2) to require a worker to take leave on a particular date or not to take leave on a particular date will continue to apply equally to accrued leave taken on the return to work. It is common for women to seek to add their leave to the end of their maternity leave in order to maximise the period off work however, this will not have the effect of extending the statutory period of maternity leave.

## Amendment to the WTR 98

Following Brexit, the Government has produced legislation designed to govern the amount and scope of law that is derived from EU Law. Under the Retained EU Law (Revocation and Reform) Act 2023 ("REULA 23") the WTR 98 are retained. However, by virtue of S2 REULA 23, s4 of the European Withdrawal Act 2018 which provided for the retention of rights, powers and liabilities under the European Communities Act 1972 is repealed from the end of 2023. The effect of that is that '*anything which, immediately before the end of 2023, is retained EU law by virtue of that section is not recognised or available in domestic law at or after that time (and, accordingly, is not to be enforced, allowed or followed).*'. In order to address this The Employment Rights (Amendment, Revocation and Transitional Provision) Regulations 2023 provide various amendments to the WTR 98. Importantly it amends Reg.13 to insert a new Reg. 13(14) which provides '*Where, as a result of taking a period of statutory leave in any leave year, a worker is unable to take some or all of the annual leave to which the worker is entitled in that leave year under this regulation, the worker is entitled to carry forward such untaken leave into the following leave year.'* Statutory leave includes ordinary and additional maternity leave. Reg. 13A is amended in equivalent terms by virtue of Reg. 13A(7A). The Department for Business & Trade has published 'Guidance – Holiday pay and entitlement reforms from 1 Jan 2024'.

## Keeping in touch

Reg. 12A MAPLE 99 addresses an employee's right to undertake work for her employer during maternity leave. These are commonly referred to as keeping in touch or 'KIT days'. Under the regulations an employee may carry out up to 10 days work for her employer without it bringing her maternity leave to an end. If any work is done on a particular day this will constitute one of the 10 days for the purposes of Reg. 12A. Work is any work done under the contract of employment and may include training or any other activity for the purposes of keeping in touch with the workplace. Reg. 12A is qualified in that none of the days can be taken in the first two weeks starting with the day that childbirth occurs ie. the period of compulsory maternity leave. Reasonable contact from time to time which either party is entitled to make will not bring maternity leave to an end. The example of reasonable contact that is given in the regulations is discussion of an employee's return to work. Importantly, the regulations do not give the right to an employer to require that work be undertaken by an employee on maternity leave or any right for an employee to be given work during the period. Any KIT days taken will not have the effect of extending the maternity leave.

## Returning to work after maternity leave

MAPLE 99 contains the notification requirements for returning from maternity leave and also set out the rights of an employee on their return. Importantly a woman's rights as to the work she returns to depend on whether she is returning from ordinary or additional maternity leave.

## Notice requirements

The assumption is that an employee will exercise her full right to ordinary and additional maternity leave unless she notifies her employer of an intention to return earlier. The notice requirements for return are contained in Reg. 11. They provide that if an employee intends to return earlier than the end of AML, she must give her employer at least eight weeks' notice of the date on which she intends to return. If an employee does not give eight weeks' notice, her employer is entitled to postpone the return to a date that will give it eight weeks' notice, however, this does not allow an employer to postpone the return beyond the end of the relevant maternity leave period. The regulations also provides for circumstances where an employee, having given the requisite eight weeks' notice, decides to return earlier than that date. In those circumstances she must give her employer at least eight weeks' notice of the new date. Similarly, if she decides to postpone her return beyond her original notified return date she must give her employer at least eight weeks' notice before the original notified date. Reg. 11 is modified for employee shareholders where the relevant notice periods are 16 weeks instead of eight (S205A ERA 96). Unlike the requirements for notifying an employer of pregnancy or the intention to take leave, Reg. 11 does not contain any requirement for an employee to give notice in writing. It is, however, advisable to put such notice in writing to avoid any dispute about whether and when notice was in fact given. An employee who returns from leave not having given the necessary notice is not entitled to be paid.

## Rights on Return

An employee who returns to work at the end of ordinary maternity leave is entitled to return to the job in which she was employed before her absence Reg. 18(1).

An employee who returns from a period of additional maternity leave or a period of ordinary leave that does not satisfy Reg. 18(1) is entitled to return to the job she was employed in before her absence *unless* it is not reasonably practicable. In those circumstances she must be permitted to return to a job which is both *suitable* and *appropriate* for her in the circumstances Reg. 18(2)).

A right to return under Reg 18(1) or (2) is a right to return with:

- Her seniority, pension rights and similar rights as they would have been if she had not been absent; and

- On terms and conditions not less favourable than those which would have applied if she had not been absent.

Reg. 18 does not apply if Reg. 10 applies (employees who are redundant during maternity leave). Reg. 10 is discussed below.

The meaning of 'job' as defined by Reg. 2(1) as *in relation to an employee returning after....maternity leave or parental leave, means the nature of the work which she is employed to do in accordance with her contract and the capacity and place in which she is so employed.*

The leading case on the interpretation of 'job' as defined in Reg. 2(1) is *Blundell v. Governing Body of St Andrew's Catholic Primary School* [2007] ICR 1451. In that case the EAT considered the application of Reg. 18(2) in the context of a primary school teacher who brought a discrimination claim pursuant to the Sex Discrimination Act 75. On return from additional maternity leave, she was given a different class to teach and therefore argued that she did not return to the job in which she was employed before her absence.

The EAT held that the contract is not definitive and the phrase 'in accordance with her contract' qualifies only the *nature* of the work and not the other two elements referred to, ie. capacity and place. Capacity is more than 'status', although it may encompass it and is a factual label, descriptive of the function which the employee serves in doing work of the nature she does. Place is also a factual label, and is not purely contractual. The question is essentially one of factual determination and judgment for the Tribunal at first instance. The EAT further held that the question should be approached having in mind firstly, the '*purposes of the legislation*' and, secondly, the fact that the regulations are for exceptional cases which provide that where it is not reasonably practicable for the employer to allow the employee to return to her previous job, he may provide for her to return to another job which is both *'suitable for her and appropriate for her to do in the circumstances'*. The EAT held that the purpose of the legislation was to seek *to ensure that there is as little dislocation as is reasonably possible in her working life, so as to avoid adding to the burdens which will inevitably exist in her family or private life simply because she has a very young infant making new demands upon her.*

It is worth considering that the original definition of 'job' in Reg. 2(1) expressly stated that it was in relation to an employee returning after 'additional' maternity leave but the word additional was removed by the Maternity and Parental Leave (Amendment) Regulations 2002 which came into force on 24th November 2002 which effectively extends the definition to meaning of job when returning from ordinary maternity leave. In the reported judgment of *Blundell* the EAT quotes the pre-amendment definition and appears to have been heavily focused on the meaning of job in the context of a return from additional maternity leave. For example, the question of whether a job is 'suitable and appropriate' should only arise in the context of a return from additional maternity leave where it is not reasonably practicable for the employer to permit an employee to return to the job in which she was employed before her absence.

'Return' means the date of return for which the employee has given the necessary notice or, the date of the end of AML. It will not matter if she does not physically return to work due to, for example, sickness or annual leave. Even if she does not physically return the return date will bring to an end the 'protected period' in relation to discrimination on the grounds of pregnancy or pregnancy related illness for the purposes of s18 EqA 10, for further discussion of pregnancy and maternity discrimination and the protected period see Chapter 8.

# CHAPTER FIVE

# PAY AND OTHER BENEFITS

## Maternity Pay

The rules surrounding qualification for maternity pay are not the same as those determining who is entitled to ordinary and maternity leave. The right to statutory maternity pay ("SMP") derives from the Social Security Contributions and Benefits Act 1992 ("SSCBA 92") and the Statutory Maternity Pay (General) Regulations 1986/60 ("SMPR 86").

A woman who qualifies for SMP, and has given the necessary notice to her employer, is entitled to a period of 39 consecutive weeks pay (Reg. 2). In summary, SMP is payable for up to 39 weeks of maternity leave.

SMP represents the minimum statutory entitlement for those who qualify. A woman may have a contractual right to more generous maternity pay. Employers who pay a higher level of contractual maternity pay usually specify that this includes the SMP amount.

## Qualification for SMP

To be entitled to SMP a woman has to satisfy the conditions set out in s164 SSCBA 92. The act uses the term 'confinement'. The definition of 'confinement' is *labour resulting in the issue of a living child, or labour after 24 weeks of pregnancy resulting in the issue of a child whether or alive or dead.* Accordingly, where the term is used, it will include a woman who has a stillbirth after 24 weeks.

The first condition is that she has been in *'employed earners employment'* for a '*continuous period of at least 26 weeks ending with the week immediately preceding the 14th week before the expected week of confinement*'. This means a woman must have been employed for at least one day of the 15th week before her baby is due ('the qualifying week'). The practical effect of the requirement for a woman to have been in continuous employment for 26 weeks before the 14th week before expected week of confinement is that an employee who is already pregnant when she commences employment will not qualify for SMP s164(2)(a).

'Employed earners employment' as it is described in s164 carries with it a wider definition than the definition of employee for the purposes of the ERA 96. In general terms it includes all those for whom an employer operates PAYE and is liable to pay national insurance. It will not cover those who are self-employed. Agency workers may be entitled to SMP from the employment agency (but not the hirer).

The second condition is that the woman's weekly earnings for the last eight weeks immediately before the 14th week before the expected week of confinement must not be less than the lower earnings limit that is in force at that time. The lower earnings limit is the current lower earnings limit for Class 1 National Insurance contributions. The rates run from 6th April each year. At the time of writing the lower earnings limit for 2023/2024 is £123 per week (gross) s164(2)(b) & s5(1)(a).

The third condition is that she has become pregnant and reached, or been confined before reaching, the start of the 11th week before the expected week of confinement s164(2)(c). This means in practice that a woman cannot ordinarily receive SMP before she is around 29 weeks pregnant unless she gives birth before then (including a still birth after 24 weeks).

Notice Requirements

A woman is only entitled to SMP if she gives the person who will be liable to pay her notice of the date from which she expects that pay to begin. The notice has to be given at least 28 days before that date or, if that is not reasonably practicable, as soon as is reasonably practicable S164(4). The notice shall be in writing if requested S164(5).

Under Reg. 22 SMPR 86, a woman must provide the employer who is liable to pay the SMP with evidence of the expected week of confinement and, where entitlement to pay depends on the fact of confinement, the week in which she gave birth. A MatB1 form will usually be sufficient for confirming the expected week of confinement and a birth certificate will be sufficient evidence of when confinement occurred.

Amount and duration of SMP

SMP is payable for up to 39 weeks in total. For the first 6 weeks an employee is entitled to 90% of her usual weekly earnings. Thereafter, she is entitled to the prescribed rate of maternity pay or her usual weekly earnings whichever is lower. The current prescribed rate can be found in Reg. 6 SMPR 86 and at the time of writing is £172.48.

Usual weekly earnings is calculated by taking the last pay date before the 'appropriate date' and the last normal pay day to fall at least 8 weeks before that appropriate date. The appropriate date is either the first day of the 14th week before the expected week of confinement or the first day in the week of confinement, whichever is earlier.

An employee can ordinarily commence maternity leave and receive SMP from the 11th week before the expected week of confinement ie. when she is approximately 29 weeks pregnant. If she gives birth before that date it will start from the day after birth. If the employee is absent at any time in the four weeks before her due date and the reason for absence is wholly or partly due to pregnancy then the maternity leave must start then. If an employee's employment ends, including by reason of dismissal by her employer, and she was employed in the 15th week before the baby was due then her (former) employer will still be obliged to pay her SMP.

## Dismissal to avoid paying SMP

S164(8) provides that regulations shall make provision as to a former employer's liability to pay SMP to a woman where her contract of service has been brought to an end by her employer solely, or mainly, for the purpose of avoiding liability for SMP. The relevant regulation is Reg. 3 SMPR 86 which provides that a former employer will be liable to pay SMP to any woman who was continuously employed for at least eight weeks and whose employment was brought to an end solely or mainly for the purpose of avoiding liability for statutory maternity pay. In addition to the employer being liable to pay the SMP, such action on their part may also give rise to a claim of automatic unfair dismissal or pregnancy and maternity discrimination which is considered in Chapters 7 & 8.

## Restrictions on contracting out

S164(6) contains an express prohibition on any agreement which either seeks to exclude, limit or otherwise modify that part of the Act or that requires an employee or former employee to contribute directly or indirectly towards any costs incurred by her employer or former employer under the Act.

Enforcement

In *Hair Division Ltd v. MacMillan* UKEAT/0033/12/BI the EAT concluded, following the analysis in *Taylor Gordon & Co Ltd v. Timmons* UKEAT/0159/03/RN, a case involving a dispute about entitlement to statutory sick pay, that the Tribunal did not have jurisdiction to determine disputes about entitlement to maternity pay. In *MacMillan* one of the issues was whether proper notice had been given under Reg. 4 MAPLE 99. Under Reg. 2 of the Statutory Sick Pay and Statutory Maternity Pay (Decisions) Regulations 1999 any application for the determination of any issue arising as to, or in connection with, entitlement to a statutory maternity pay may be submitted to an officer of the Board (HMRC) by an employee. The conditions for such an application are that:

- It is made in writing
- It is sent within 6 months of the earliest date the pay became in issue
- It states the period for which entitlement is in issue; and
- It states the grounds (if any) on which the employer has denied liability for the pay in respect of the period specified in the application

HMRC advise that in such circumstances you should contact the Statutory Payment Dispute Team whose up-to-date phone number and address can be found online on their Gov.Uk web page.

A determination as to the entitlement to SMP is subject to the right to appeal but, once the time for appealing the determination has expired (or no appeal has been lodged), then Reg. 7 SMPR 86 provides that the payments that have been determined to be owing will be the liability of the Commissioners of Inland Revenue and not the employer. The first payment should be made as soon as reasonably practicable after the liability arises and should then be made weekly (Reg. 30).

For employers it is important to be aware of s113A(6) of the Social Security Administration Act 1992 which exposes an employer to the risk of a fine of up to £3000 if they refuse, or repeatedly fail, to pay maternity pay.

In *MacMillan,* the tribunal did observe that SMP falls within the definition of wages within the ERA 96 for the purposes of an unlawful deduction from wages claim but drew a distinction between deciding the issue of whether SMP has or has not been paid and the question of entitlement to SMP in the first place. In many cases the latter will be in dispute and it will usually be sensible to pursue any such claim via HMRC rather than a tribunal wages claim.

Non-payment of SMP may give rise to other claims such as a detriment claim or a constructive automatically unfair dismissal claim under ERA 96 which is discussed further in Chapters 6 and 7.

## Maternity Allowance

Those who do not qualify for SMP, for example by virtue of their employment status, or because they did not have sufficient qualifying service with their current employer, may be able to claim maternity allowance ('MA'). MA is not paid by the employer. To qualify for MA a woman must satisfy the requirements of s35(1) SSCB 92. Namely:

- She has become pregnant and reached 11 weeks before the expected week of childbirth. Like SMP, MA can be paid if birth occurs at an earlier date including a stillbirth after 24 weeks

- She has been employed or self-employed for a minimum of 26 weeks in the 66 weeks before the expected week of childbirth. The weeks do not need to have been consecutive weeks and it will be sufficient if she has worked any part of the week

- Her average weekly earnings are not less than the maternity allowance threshold for the tax year in which the beginning of the 66-week period begins. The threshold is currently £30

- She is not entitled to SMP for the same week for the same pregnancy

MA lasts for 39 weeks and it is at the prescribed rate (currently £172.48) or 90% of average earnings (whichever is lower) for the entire period.

# CHAPTER SIX

# PROTECTION FROM DETRIMENT

Part V ERA 96

Part V ERA 96 deals with the protection against suffering a detriment in employment. In particular, s47C ERA 96 deals with detriment in relation to leave for family and domestic reasons which provides that an employee has the right not to be subjected to any detriment by any act, or failure to act by employer done for a prescribed reason. Prescribed reasons are ones which are prescribed in regulations and relate to:

- Pregnancy, childbirth or maternity
- Time off to accompany a pregnant employee to an antenatal appointment (S57ZE)
- Time off to attend adoption appointments (S57ZJ & s57ZL)
- Ordinary, compulsory or additional maternity leave
- Ordinary or additional adoption leave
- Shared parental leave
- Parental leave
- Paternity leave
- Parental bereavement leave

- Time off for dependents (s57A)

As can be seen, the matters that fall within s47C are broad and derive from a number of regulations. For the purposes of pregnancy and maternity the principal regulation is Reg. 19 MAPLE 99 which provides that an employee is entitled under section 47C of the 1996 Act *not to be subjected to any detriment by any act, or any deliberate failure to act, by her employer done for any of the reasons specified in paragraph (2)*. The reasons in paragraph (2) are that the employee:

- Is pregnant
- Has given birth to a child
- Is subject of a relevant requirement or recommendation under s66(2) ERA 96 ie. suspension on maternity grounds
- Took, sought to take or availed herself of the benefits of ordinary or additional maternity leave
- Took or sought to take parental leave or time off for dependents
- Failed to return to work after a period of maternity leave where the employer had failed to give the required notice of the end date of the leave and the employee reasonably believed the period had not ended or the employer gave her less than 28 days' notice of when the period will end and it was not reasonably practicable to return on that date.
- Undertook, considered undertaking or refused to undertake work in accordance with Reg. 12A (KIT days)
- Declined to sign a workforce agreement for the purposes of the regulations

- Being a workplace representative for the purposes of Schedule 1 or being a candidate in an election to be such a representative performed or proposed to perform functions or activities as a representative or candidate.

The other relevant regulations which contain prescribed reasons under S47C are Paternity and Adoption Leave Regulations 2002 (PALR 02), the Shared Parental Leave Regulations 2014 (SPLR 14) and the Parental Bereavement Regulations 2020 (PBR 20).

S47C(1) protects employees from being subjected to a detriment for the reasons listed above. Employee means an employee that falls within the definition of s230 ERA 96. There is no qualifying period of employment and it is not in general confined to a protected period equivalent to that found in S18 EqA 10 however, the specific ground of 'has given birth to a child' *is* limited by Reg. 19(5) which provides that it only applies where the act or failure to act takes place during the employee's ordinary or additional maternity leave period.

The prohibition on subjecting an employee to a detriment because she has taken, sought to take or availed herself of the benefits of ordinary or additional maternity leave is further clarified in Reg. 19(3) and (3A) which provide that she avails herself of the benefits of ordinary or additional maternity leave if she avails herself of any of the terms and conditions of her employment preserved by s71 (ordinary maternity leave) and s73 (additional maternity leave) and Reg. 9 during that period.

S47C(5) also provides more limited protection for agency workers within the meaning of the Agency Workers Regulations 2010 from the temporary work agency and the hirer in relation to exercising their rights to attend ante natal care appointments and receive remuneration ( s57ZA & s57ZB), time off to accompany to ante natal appointments (s57ZG) and time off for adoptions appointments and meetings (s57ZN, S57ZO and s57ZP).

## Detriment

In common with the other provisions of Part V, s47C and its associated regulations, do not provide a definition of what is meant by detriment. However, the concept is understood to have the same meaning across the provisions of Part V and indeed to be analogous with the concept as contained in S39 EqA 10.

In *Shamoon v. Chief Constable of the Royal Ulster Constabulary* [2003] IRLR 285 the question of detriment was considered by the House of Lords in the context of direct sex discrimination. In that case it was held that a detriment would be something that a reasonable worker would or might take the view was a disadvantage. It was not necessary to demonstrate some physical or economic consequence. However, an unjustified sense of grievance would not amount to a detriment.

The question of detriment was considered by the Court of Appeal in the context of the ERA 96 in the whistle-blowing claim of *Jesudason v. Alder Hey Children's NHS Foundation Trust* [2020] IRLR 374 which confirmed that the concept of detriment in cases such as *Shamoon* had the same meaning in whistleblowing cases. In that case, it was noted that some workers may not consider that particular treatment amounts to a detriment; they may be unconcerned about it and not consider themselves to be prejudiced or disadvantaged in any way but, if a reasonable worker might do so, that the claimant genuinely does so, is enough. The test therefore is not wholly objective.

Detriment, in the context of pregnancy and maternity, can arise in a number of ways, examples might include failures to inform or consult employees about matters when they are on maternity leave or failing to offer opportunities to employees who are pregnant or on maternity leave. It should be noted however, that it will not be a detriment for an employer to have acted in accordance with statute and the regulations. In *Hoyland v. Asda Stores Ltd* [2005] ICR 1235 the EAT rejected an appeal brought by an employee in relation to the fact that she had not been paid a bonus due to the fact that she had been on maternity leave.

The bonus was to reflect work done for a period when she had not been at work. The sum was payable by way of wages or salary and, therefore, fell within the exclusion contained in Reg. 9 that provides that an employee is not entitled to the benefit of terms and conditions relating to remuneration during ordinary and additional maternity leave. It was observed that to find otherwise would render the regulations meaningless.

Although a detriment may prove relatively easy to establish the employee will still need to establish the 'causation' element. The right under s47C is the right not to be 'be subjected to any detriment' by 'any act or failure to act' by her employer done for a prescribed reason. Further, the regulations specify that in relation to maternity leave that the detriment must be because she took or sought to take or availed herself of the benefits of maternity leave. As with the meaning of detriment, guidance on causation can be derived from other types of detriment cases under Part V ERA 96, particularly in relation to whistleblowing which has received a relatively high degree of scrutiny at appellate level. Another fertile area has been the prohibition of detriment in relation to Trade Union Activities found in s146 Trade Union & Labour Relations (Consolidation) Act 1992 ("TULCRA 92"). It will not simply be enough to point to the fact that the employee possesses a characteristic that is protected under s47C, eg. the fact that they are on maternity leave, and that a detriment has been suffered to establish that this is the reason for the treatment. In the same way motive is not relevant in the discrimination context the employer's motive will not matter for a detriment claim. This can arise, for example, if an employer wrongly thinks they are acting in a way that is beneficial to an employee. An example might be not informing the employee about an important work matter because they are on maternity leave. If the failure to inform was a detriment then the fact that the employer might believe it was better not to disturb an employee on maternity leave would not mean that it wasn't on that prohibited ground. There is one important caveat as to what can amount to a detriment and that is that, in common with the other provisions which prohibit an employer subjected an employee to a detriment on specific grounds, dismissal is specifically excluded (Reg. 19(4) MAPLE 99). Dismissal is dealt with in Chapter 7.

The question of the degree to which the prohibited reason needed to have been part of the reason for the act or failure to act was considered by the Court of Appeal in the whistleblowing case of *Fecitt and ors and Public Concern At Work v. NHS Manchester* [2012] IRLR 64. The Court of Appeal, disagreeing with the EAT, held that the test for detriment in a s47B claim was *not* whether the treatment was 'in no sense whatsoever' on the grounds that the Claimant had made a protected disclosure but whether the protected disclosure materially influences (in the sense of being more than a trivial influence) the employer's treatment of the whistleblower. This was notwithstanding that it created the curious situation that the test for whistleblowing dismissal under s103A requires the protected disclosure to be the sole or principal reason for the dismissal. This same situation arises in relation to s47C and s99 which provides for automatic unfair dismissal if the reason or principal reason for dismissal is on proscribed grounds relating to leave for family reasons which is explored further in Chapter 7. *Fecitt* also confirmed that s47B as then worded did not allow for an employer to be vicariously liable for the acts of victimisation of its employees where the employees had committed no legal wrong. S47B was subsequently amended to address this issue. S47C has not been amended in the same way however, employers can, of course, be vicariously liable for a discrimination claim under the Equality Act 2010.

It Is also important to be aware of the specific issue of the burden of proof in relation to detriment claims. This derives from s48 ERA 96 which conveys jurisdiction on the Tribunal to hear complaints of detriment under Part V. S48(2) provides that on a complaint under s48(1) (which includes a s47C claim) that it is for the employer to show the ground on which any act, or deliberate failure to act was done. This is sometimes expressed as meaning the burden of proof is on the employer. Applying s48(2) if an employee can show there has been a detriment and the employer has subjected the employee to that detriment the Tribunal will then look to the employer for an explanation. The primary burden still rests with the Claimant to show that a detriment occurred *Hollinghurst v. James Hall & Co Ltd* UKEAT 0162/17. However, if detriment is established and an employer is looked to for an explanation that does not mean that unless the employer can show a positive reason why any action (or inaction) was taken that the employee's complaint must succeed. In the case of *Kuzel v. Roche Products Ltd* [2008] ICR 799 the Court of Appeal considered the position in relation to a complaint of automatically unfair dismissal under s103A ERA 96. In that case, allowing the employers cross appeal, they held that if a Tribunal rejected an employers stated reason for dismissal they may accept the reason contended for by the employee (in this case that she had made a protected disclosure) but were not bound to do so and in that case the Tribunal had been entitled to conclude that the reason was not the one contended for by either side. That principle was subsequently applied by the EAT in the context of a detriment claim in *Mrs J Ibekwe v. Sussex Partnership NHS Foundation Trust* UKEAT/0072/14/MC.

## Enforcement

As highlighted above, the Tribunal has jurisdiction to hear complaints of detriment under s47C by virtue of s48. The time limit for presenting such a complaint is 3 months from the date of the act or failure to act or the last in a serious of acts. A complaint under s48 is subject to a requirement to undertake ACAS early conciliation. The test for whether the Tribunal has jurisdiction for a claim that is not presented in time is the reasonable practicability test.

S49 sets out the remedies that are available. If a Tribunal finds a claim is well founded then they must make a declaration to that effect. They may make an award of financial compensation of an amount they consider just and equitable having regard to the infringement and loss which is attributable to the act or failure to act. Loss includes expenses reasonably incurred and the loss of any benefit that the employee might reasonably have expected to have but for the act of failure to act. The employee is under a duty to mitigate their losses and the Tribunal may make a reduction for contributory conduct. The Tribunal may make an award of injury to feelings in respect of a detriment claim. There is no separate guidance for detriment claims and the Tribunal will generally use the *Vento* guidelines to assist them to arrive at a figure for injury to feelings. The current *Vento* guidance is set out in Chapter 8.

# CHAPTER SEVEN

# DISMISSAL

## Automatic Unfair Dismissal

S99 ERA 96 makes a dismissal unfair where the reason, or principal reason, for the dismissal is of a prescribed kind relating to Leave for Family Reasons *or* takes place in prescribed circumstances. If s99 is satisfied the dismissal is automatically unfair without the need for further consideration. S99(2) states that a reason is a prescribed one if it is prescribed by regulations. S99(3) states that the reason or set of circumstances must relate to:

- Pregnancy, childbirth or maternity
- Time off to accompany a pregnant employee to an antenatal appointment (S57ZE)
- Time off to attend adoption appointments (S57ZJ & s57ZL)
- Ordinary, compulsory or additional maternity leave
- Ordinary or additional adoption leave
- Shared parental leave
- Parental leave
- Paternity leave
- Parental bereavement leave
- Time off for dependents (s57A)

It may also relate to redundancy or other factors which is discussed further below. The relevant regulation which prescribes the reason or circumstances for the purposes of S99(2) in respect of pregnancy and maternity is Reg. 20 MAPLE. Reg. 20 provides that an employee who is dismissed shall be considered unfairly dismissed for the purposes of Part X ERA 96 if the reason is connected with one of the following:

- The pregnancy of the employee
- The fact that the employee has given birth to a child
- The application of a relevant requirement or recommendation under s66(2) ERA 96 ie suspension on maternity grounds
- The fact that she took, sought to take or availed herself of the benefits of ordinary or additional maternity leave
- Took or sought to take parental leave or time off for dependents
- The fact she failed to return to work after a period of maternity leave where the employer
    - had failed to give the required notice of the end date of the leave and the employee reasonably believed the period had not ended, or
    - the employer gave her less than 28 days' notice of when the period will end and it was not reasonably practicable to return on that date.
- The fact that she undertook, considered undertaking or refused to undertake work in accordance with Reg 12A (KIT days)
- The fact she declined to sign a workforce agreement for the purposes of the regulations

- The fact that the employee being a workplace representative for the purposes of Schedule 1 or, being a candidate in an election to be such a representative performed or proposed to perform functions or activities as a representative or candidate

Similarly to the provisions of Reg. 19 (protection from detriment, discussed in Chapter 6 above), 'has given birth to a child' is a time limited prohibited reason if the dismissal ends the employee's ordinary or additional maternity leave period. The prohibition on dismissing the employee because she has taken, sought to take or availed herself of the benefits of ordinary or additional maternity leave is defined by reference to Reg. 19(3) and (3A) which provide that she avails herself of the benefits of ordinary or additional maternity leave if she avails herself of any of the terms and conditions of her employment preserved by s71 (ordinary maternity leave) and s73 (additional maternity leave) and Reg. 9 during that period (Reg. 3(5)).

Pursuant to Reg. 20(1)(b) an employee will be regarded as unfairly dismissed for the purposes of Part X if the reason or principal reason for the dismissal is that the employee is redundant, that dismissal ends an employee's ordinary or additional maternity leave, and Reg. 10 has not been complied with. Reg. 10 is examined in more detail below.

Reg. 20(2) provides that an employee will be unfairly dismissed if the reason or principle reason is that:

- The employee was redundant and it is shown that;
    - The circumstances constituting the redundancy applied equally to one or more employees in the same undertaking who held positions similar to that held by the employee and who have not been dismissed; and
    - it is shown that the reason or, if more than one, the principle reason the employee was selected was a reason

listed within Reg 20(3).

Finally, Reg. 20(7) provides that the employee will not be unfairly dismissed pursuant to Reg. 20(1) if;

- It is not reasonably practicable for a reason other than redundancy for the employer to permit her to return to a job which is both suitable for her and appropriate for her to do in the circumstances;

- An associated employer offers her a job of that kind, and

- She accepts or unreasonably refuses that offer.

The reference to a job which is both suitable and appropriate is the same as the language used in Reg. 18 regarding an employee's right to return to work after additional maternity leave the meaning of which is discussed in more detail in Chapter 4.

The other relevant regulations which contain prescribed reasons under S99 ERA 96 are Paternity and Adoption Leave Regulations 2002 (PALR 02), the Shared Parental Leave Regulations 2014 (SPLR 14) and the Parental Bereavement Regulations 2020 (PBR 20).

## Meaning of Dismissal

The definition of dismissal is contained in s95 ERA 96 and applies both to 'ordinary' and 'automatically' unfair dismissal. This includes a termination by the employer with or without notice, a limited term contract which terminates by virtue of the limiting event without being renewed (eg. a fixed term contract) and where an employee terminates her contract with or without notice in circumstances in which she is entitled to terminate without notice because of the employer's conduct ie. constructive dismissal.

Qualifying Employment

One of the important differences between s98 (ordinary unfair dismissal) and s99 automatic unfair dismissal is that the requirement contained in s108 for an employee to have been continuously employed for two years at the effective date of termination in order to be able to bring a complaint of unfair dismissal does not apply to automatic unfair dismissals including s99 ERA 96.

Burden of Proof

The employee's length of service does, however, have some impact on the burden of proof. Under s98, ordinary unfair dismissal, the burden rests on the employer to show that the employee was dismissed for a potentially fair reason within the meaning of s98(2). Where an employee has qualifying service for a claim of ordinary unfair dismissal and is asserting that the reason for the dismissal was not a potentially fair one but, in fact, for an automatically unfair reason if the employer produces some evidence appearing to show the reason for the dismissal then the burden shifts to the employee to demonstrate that there is a genuine issue as to the reason for the dismissal *Maund v. Penwith DC* [1984] ICR 143. However, as the Court of Appeal confirmed in *Maund,* which was a case where the Claimant alleged he had been dismissed for Trade Union Activities and not redundancy as contended by the employer, the burden does not shift to the employee to prove the reason for dismissal. It is an evidential burden, once the employee shows some evidence that puts doubt on the employer's reason the burden of proof remains on the employer. As was established in *Kuzel v. Roche Products Ltd* [2008] ICR 799 which considered *Maund,* it does not follow that if the Tribunal rejects the employer's stated reason for dismissal or detriment it is bound to find it was for the prohibited reason asserted by the employee (although it often might). Of course, a key difference between a detriment and dismissal claim is that for a dismissal claim the prohibited reason needs to be the reason or, if more than one reason, the principal reason for the dismissal whereas something lesser is needed for a detriment claim (see Chapter 6) If however, an employee does not have the qualifying service and can only make a claim of automatically unfair dismissal the burden will rest on her to show that the reason for dismissal was for the prohibited reason. This principal was first stated in the majority decision of the Court of Appeal in *Smith v. Hayle Town Council* [1978] ICR 996 in a case involving allegations that the reason for dismissal was on Trade Union Grounds and has been applied in the context of automatic unfair dismissal under Part X ERA 96 in cases such as the EAT decision of *Ross v. Eddie Stobart Ltd* UKEAT/0068/13 which concerned a complaint of automatic unfair dismissal for whistleblowing under s103A.

Reason for Dismissal

When considering whether the decision to dismiss has been made on grounds proscribed by s99 ERA 96 the starting point is the classic definition of the reason for dismissal stated by Cairns LJ in *Abernethy v. Mott, Hay and Anderson* [1974] ICR 323

> *'A reason for the dismissal of an employee is a set of facts known to the employer, or it may be of beliefs held by him, which cause him to dismiss the employee'*

In the context of a dismissal alleged to be because the employee is pregnant there will generally need to be knowledge of the pregnancy on the part of the employer. However, that does not mean that the employee must have expressly informed her employer of her pregnancy. A belief on the part of the employer will be sufficient *Ramdoolar v. Bycity Ltd* [2005] ICR 368. In *Ramdoolar* the Tribunal rejected the employee's claim that she had expressly informed her employer of her pregnancy and consequently dismissed her complaint under Reg. 20(3)(a) MAPLE 99. The Tribunal had applied the principles set out in *Del Monte Foods v. Mundan* [1980] ICR 694 which had held it was essential that the employer knew or believed that the Claimant was pregnant. Some doubt had been cast on the EAT conclusions as to knowledge in *Ramdoolar* by Lindsay J in the later case of *H J Heinz Ltd v. Kenrick* [2000] ICR 491. In *Ramdoolar* it was argued on behalf of the employee that if an employer ought, by reason of symptoms or behaviour displayed by the employee, to have known that she was pregnant, then, if he dismissed her for a reason that in fact turned out to be connected with her pregnancy, the dismissal is automatically unfair. After a careful review of the authorities and the statutory regime the EAT rejected this contention and confirmed the position as established in *Mundan* with one possible qualification. The qualification was that the EAT recognised that there could potentially be circumstances where the employer detected symptoms of pregnancy and fearing the consequences dismissed the employee before their suspicions could be proved right. In those circumstances it may well be that the dismissal was automatically unfair.

## Relevance of the Decision Maker

In Chapter 8 the relevance of the decision maker is examined in the context of a s18 EqA 10 discrimination claim in light of the recent EAT case of *Alcedo Orange Limited v. Ferridge-Gunn* EA-2022-000775-JOJ. In relation to unfair dismissal claims under the ERA 96 it is necessary to have regard to the Supreme Court decision in the whistleblowing case of *Royal Mail v. Jhuti* [2020] ICR 731. In *Jhuti* the employee made protected disclosures to her manager, W, as a result of those disclosures he subjected her to detriments in the form of unwarranted performance management. An 'innocent' manager was tasked with considering whether Mrs Jhuti should be dismissed on performance grounds. Mrs Jhuti was too unwell to participate in the exercise and the decision maker genuinely believed on the evidence presented to her that there were performance issues. In the Supreme Court it was held that where a person in the hierarchy of responsibility above the employee determines that she should be dismissed for a reason but hides it behind an invented reason which the decision-maker adopts, the reason for the dismissal is the hidden reason rather than the invented reason. It was observed, however, that the facts giving rise to such a scenario would be rare.

'Connected with'

Reg 20(3) requires that the reason for the dismissal is '*connected with*' one of the matters set out in the regulations. The meaning of 'connected with' was considered in *Clayton v. Vigers* [1989] ICR 713. In that case a dental nurse was dismissed while on maternity leave on the grounds that her employer had been unable to secure a temporary replacement and had therefore employed a permanent employee. The EAT considered s60 of the Employment Protection (Consolidation) Act 1978 which provided that a dismissal was unfair if the reason or principal reason was that an employee was pregnant or was any other reason connected with pregnancy. The EAT concluded that the background to the decision to dismiss was the pregnancy or the after-effects of the pregnancy which was part of the reason for the dismissal and any other reason connected to pregnancy should be read widely to give full effect at the mischief at which the statute was aimed. S99 ERA 96 and Reg. 20 now expressly deal with maternity leave which was the 'after-effect' of pregnancy with which *Clayton* was concerned.

Another common issue that arises in the context of whether the reason for dismissal is 'connected with' pregnancy is the question of dismissal for illness which is said to have arisen as a result of pregnancy. In *Caledonia Bureau of Investment and property v. Caffrey* [1998] ICR 603 an employee was unable to return to work at the expiry of her maternity leave due to post-natal depression and was dismissed after six weeks. The EAT held that if a pregnancy related illness which had arisen during an employee's maternity leave was a direct cause of her dismissal then it was unfair under s99 ERA 96. The EAT also found that it was direct sex discrimination under the then relevant provisions of the Sex

Discrimination Act 1975. *Caffrey* was considered in *Lyons v. DWP Jobcentre Plus* [2014] ICR 668. *Lyons* was concerned with an employee who had been dismissed after being unable to return to work after maternity leave due to post-natal depression. The Tribunal found that she was unfairly dismissed pursuant to s98 ERA 96 but rejected her claims of discrimination under s13 and s18 EqA 10. On appeal it was observed that *Caffrey* had been decided before the judgment in *Brown v. Rentokil* [1998] ICR 790 and prior to the amendment of the SDA 75, for further discussion of *Brown* see Chapter 8. The EAT held that the Tribunal had been correct not to follow *Caffrey* and to reject her claim of discrimination. In particular, her claim under s18 failed as the dismissal had taken place due to absence outside the protected period. However, although noting the finding of unfair dismissal under s99 ERA 96 in *Caffrey* this did not form part of the appeal in *Lyons* and was not commented on substantively by the EAT and arguably remains good authority on the point. This appeared to create a situation where the protection in relation to pregnancy related illness is arguably more extensive under the ERA 96 than section 18 because it can extend to acts which occur after the end of maternity leave. It is worth noting that the decision in *Caffrey* has also been questioned as to its characterisation of post-natal depression as a pregnancy related illness as opposed to an illness arising from the fact that the employee has given birth. If it was the latter then arguably the limitation of reg. 20(4) would mean that it would only be unfair if the dismissal brought the maternity leave to an end. For more detailed discussion of s18 EqA 10, the meaning of the protected period and recent amendments to the Equality Act see Chapter 8.

## Redundancy

Reg. 20 MAPLE 99 provides two distinct protections in relation to an employee who is made redundant whilst pregnant or on maternity leave:

- Reg. 20(1)(b) provides that an employee is unfairly dismissed if the reason or principal reason for the dismissal is that the employee is redundant and Reg. 10 has not been complied with

- Reg. 20(2) provides that an employee will be unfairly dismissed if:

    - The reason (or, if more than one the principal reason) for which she is dismissed is that she was redundant;

    - It is shown that the circumstances constituting the redundancy applied equally to one of more employees in the same undertaking who held positions similar to that held by the employee and who have not been dismissed by the employer; and

    - It is shown that the reason (or, if more than one the principal reason) for which the employee was selected was a reason of a kind specified in Reg. 20(3)

These two provisions are considered in turn below.

<u>Reg. 20(1)(b) and Reg. 10 MAPLE 99</u>

Reg. 10 provides an important and specific protection to women on ordinary or additional maternity leave who are redundant. Reg. 10 requires that if a woman is on OML or AML and it is not practicable by reason of redundancy for an employer to continue to employ her under her existing contract of employment and there is a suitable available vacancy then she is entitled to be offered that vacancy before the end of her employment. The vacancy can be with the employer, its successor or an associated employer. The new contract of employment must be for work that is both suitable for the employee and appropriate for her to do in the circumstances. The terms and conditions including the capacity for which she is employed and the location must not be substantially less favourable than if she had remained employed on her previous contract.

Redundancy for the purposes of MAPLE 99 has the same meaning as the definition of redundancy in s139 ERA 96 ie. where the requirements of the business for employees to carry out work of a particular kind has ceased or diminished, or are expected to case or diminish *Secretary of State for Justice v. Slee* UKEAT/0349/06/JOJ.

In *Sefton Borough Council v. Wainwright* UKEAT/0168/14/LA_the EAT considered the question of timing as to when the obligations under Reg. 10 arose. In that case the employer argued that the obligations under Reg. 10 had not arisen until after another displaced employee had been slotted into the suitable vacancy. The EAT rejected this argument and upheld the Tribunal's finding that the obligations had arisen once the decision had been made that the Claimant's post would be deleted. To adopt the employer's proposed approach would be to undermine the protection of Reg. 10. Once the employee's position is redundant within the meaning of the definition the obligation arose.

The meaning of available vacancy was considered in *Community Task Force v. Rimmer* [1986] ICR 491. Availability is a question of fact and is not qualified by consideration of what is 'economic or reasonable'. If the vacancy is available the consequences for the employer giving the job are irrelevant. In that case the vacancy in question was meant for someone who was long-term unemployed and to give the vacancy to the Claimant risked the employer losing funding. Nonetheless, it was an available vacancy.

Whether the vacancy is suitable is a matter for assessment by the employer. For a vacancy to be suitable it must both satisfy the test of appropriateness and not be substantially less favourable in relation to the terms and conditions *Simpson v. Endsleigh Insurance Services Ltd and ors* UKEAT/0544/09/DA.

Reg. 10 is not without its limits. In *Eversheds Legal Services v. De Belin*

[2011] IRLR 448, the EAT held that the obligation is to do what is reasonably necessary to afford the statutory protection to the woman who is pregnant or on maternity leave, doing more than reasonably necessary would be disproportionate and puts the employer at risk of unlawfully discriminating against others. In *De Belin* the EAT upheld a finding that a male employee had been subject to sex discrimination when he had been selected for redundancy based on a female employee having been given the maximum score on one of the selection criteria because she had been on maternity leave for the relevant period of measuring that criteria. The employer had proceeded on the basis it was obliged to operate the selection in that way. In *Sefton,* the EAT accepted the Respondent's submission that Reg. 10 does not define vacancy and does not expressly oblige an employer to offer every suitable vacancy. In *Sefton* it was clear that the employer considered the male employee at risk to be much more suitable for the role and the EAT observed that if the Respondent, had, as a matter of fact, offered another suitable vacancy to the Claimant that might well have complied with Reg 10.

A recent example of the difficulties an employer potentially faces in a having to grapple with the issue of Reg 10, S18 and the effect of *De Belin* can be seen in *Hunter v. Carnival Plc* ET Case No: 1401917/2021. In that case the Claimant was employed as a Team leader for the Respondent. While she was on maternity leave the Respondent undertook a redundancy exercise whereby the number of Team Leader roles was to be reduced from 21 to 16. The selection was undertaken by a scoring exercise that put the Claimant in the bottom five and she was made redundant. The Tribunal considered *Sefton* and *De Belin.* The Respondent relying on *De Belin* argued that they had been entitled to use the pool in order to determine who would be *selected* for redundancy and that there were no suitable vacancies within the meaning of Reg. 10 until that exercise was undertaken. The Tribunal found that the Claimant was 'at risk' of redundancy as soon as the consultation exercise commenced. The Respondent put everyone at risk and created a set number of vacancies, any of those vacancies was suitable for the Claimant. The dismissal was therefore automatically unfair under Reg. 10. This reasoning is a little difficult to reconcile with *De Belin* and arguably the Tribunal wrongly treated being 'at risk' of redundancy as triggering Reg. 10 or, rather artificially, treated the employer's decision to reduce the number of posts as analogous to the 'deletion' of the post as was found to have occurred in *Sefton*. In this case the Tribunal may have found their decision somewhat easier as they also found that the Claimant's scoring had been adversely affected by the fact that she was on maternity leave and found, in the alternative, that she had been automatically unfairly dismissed under Reg 20.(2) (see below) and that this was an ordinary unfair dismissal in any event. However, if the Claimant had been scored objectively fairly and been given one of the 16 roles at the expense of a higher scoring man it must be considered that the employer may have been vulnerable if he had brought a claim of sex discrimination.

A breach of Reg. 10 may also be an act of pregnancy and maternity discrimination but not necessarily so. A breach of Reg. 10 does not mean there is inherent discrimination. In *Sefton* the EAT found that the Tribunal had erred in assuming the question of whether there had been discrimination under s18 EqA 10 had been answered by its finding that there had been a breach of Reg. 10. In many cases the S18 discrimination question may be answered by a finding of breach under Reg. 10 but the Tribunal must always answer the question of what was the reason for the treatment. The Tribunal in *Hunter* heeding EAT guidance in *Sefton* did not find the Claimant's dismissal was also discriminatory. For further discussion of causation in discrimination cases see Chapter 8.

Reg 20(2) MAPLE 99

Reg. 20(2) provides protection for an employee in a genuine redundancy situation where the reason why she is selected for redundancy is connected with one of the reasons set out in Reg. 20(3) which are that the employee:

- Is pregnant
- Has given birth to a child
- Is subject of a relevant requirement or recommendation under s66(2) ERA 96 ie. suspension on maternity grounds
- Took, sought to take or availed herself of the benefits of ordinary or additional maternity leave
- Took or sought to take parental leave or time off for dependents
- Failed to return to work after a period of maternity leave where the employer had failed to give the required notice of the end date of the leave and the employee reasonably believed the period had not ended or the employer gave her less than 28 days' notice of when the period will end and it was not reasonably practicable to return on that date.
- Undertook, considered undertaking or refused to undertake work in accordance with Reg. 12A (KIT days)
- Declined to sign a workforce agreement for the purposes of the regulations
- Being a workplace representative for the purposes of Schedule 1 or being a candidate in an election to be such a representative performed or proposed to perform functions or activities as a representative or candidate.

The application of Reg. 20 in the context of redundancy was considered by the EAT in *S G Petch Ltd v. English-Stewart* UKEAT/0213/12. In that case an employee was dismissed following her maternity leave in circumstances where her employer argued that the fact of her maternity leave had revealed that her role was redundant as they had been able to absorb her work without employing a replacement. The Tribunal had concluded that she was dismissed on the grounds that she had taken maternity leave and this was automatically unfair applying Reg. 20(1). The EAT found that the Tribunal had, in fact, made a finding that the Claimant's role was redundant and the Tribunal should therefore have considered the dismissal under Reg 20(2) instead of Reg 20(1) (It appears that Reg. 10 did not apply in this case as she was not on maternity leave). The EAT then went on to consider whether, based on the Tribunal's findings the three elements of Reg 20(2) had been made out, namely:

- She was redundant
- The circumstances applied equally to other employees in similar positions who had not been made redundant
- The reason was connected to one of the reasons in 20(3)

The EAT had already concluded that the Tribunal had found there was a redundancy situation. On the issue of whether it was connected with a reason in Reg 20(3) they observed:

> *The question can simply be put, described as a "coincidental" decision by the employer in the letter that we referred to in para 15 above: namely, where it becomes apparent, as was accepted, during the maternity leave that there is a redundancy position, i.e. that the job of the person on maternity leave is superfluous to requirements, then is a decision so reached one that can be said to be, and indeed is, connected with the maternity leave? In the course of argument we put the following suggestion: that if in fact it is not connected with*

> *maternity leave, then there is a real problem for a woman taking maternity leave that it may turn out in her absence not simply that someone else is better at the job than she but that her job itself is unnecessary, because it does not need to be carried on by anybody in her absence, thus revealing a redundancy situation such as was the case here. It appears to us that it must be that such a position falls within the rubric "connected with maternity leave".*

They noted that in this case it had been stated by the employer that the situation would have arisen and that the same discussions (about the lack of need for the role) would have taken place regardless of her absence on maternity leave. The EAT said that if it was the case that the redundancy situation could have or had been appreciated irrespective of the maternity leave then it was possible that on those facts that it was not connected, however, that was no such evidence in the present case. The EAT were however, unable to address the issue of whether the other employees had been in similar positions to the Claimant (who had been the manager of the remaining three employees). They therefore remitted this question to the Tribunal. The EAT also found that the Tribunal had erred in concluding the Claimant had been discriminated against and dismissed that claim without remission.

ACAS Guidance

ACAS in conjunction with the EHRC have produced a guide for employers entitled 'Managing redundancy for pregnant employees or those on maternity leave'. It was last revised in 2018 and contains a number of practical examples of potential scenarios and a myth busting section. It is a useful tool for an employer contemplating redundancy.

Future Developments

On 24th July 2023 the Protection from Redundancy (Pregnancy and Family Leave) Act 2023 came into force. The intention of the Act, amongst other things, is to extend protection in relation to redundancy to pregnant employees and to extend it to a period after they return from maternity leave. The act provides for these further protections to be provided by way of regulations made by the Secretary of State including provision for a 'protected period'. At the time of writing draft regulations have been laid before parliament entitled Maternity Leave, Adoption Leave and Shared Parental Leave (Amendment) Regulations 2024. Reg.4 extends the protection contained in Reg. 10(1) MAPLE 99 from ordinary or additional maternity leave to cover:

- The protected period of pregnancy
- The statutory maternity leave period; or
- The additional protected period

The protected period will start on the day the employer is informed of the pregnancy (which could be after the end of the pregnancy) and will end on the day the statutory maternity period commences. If the employee does not have a right to statutory maternity leave then the period will end at the end of two weeks after the end of the pregnancy. The additional protected period will cover 18 months from the expected week of childbirth (or actual date of childbirth if the employer is notified).

## Other dismissal claims

In addition to a claim of automatic unfair dismissal pursuant to s99 ERA 96, there are two further points to note.

The first is that subject to qualifying employment, regardless of whether a dismissal is automatically unfair it may, in any event, be ordinary unfair dismissal and those advising Claimants would be well advised to make clear in any pleadings that a claim of unfair dismissal is put on both the ordinary and automatic unfair dismissal basis.

The second is that in addition to S99, s104 ERA 96 makes it automatically unfair to dismiss an employee for asserting a statutory right. S104 provides that an employee will be automatically unfairly dismissed if the reason (or, if more than one, the principal reason) is that the employee brought proceedings against an employer to enforce a right which is a relevant statutory right or alleged that the employer had infringed a relevant statutory right. It does not matter for the purposes of s104 whether the employee in fact has the right or whether it has in fact been infringed but the claim must have been made in good faith. The meaning of statutory right is broad and includes any right conferred by the ERA 96 for which the remedy for its infringement is by way of complaint or reference to an employment tribunal.

## Complaints to Tribunal

S111 gives the Tribunal jurisdiction to hear complaints of both ordinary and automatic unfair dismissal. The requirements of ACAS early conciliation apply and the time limit subject to any extension is three months from the effective date of termination. The test if a complaint is presented outside the ordinary time limit is one of reasonable practicability.

## Remedy

If the Tribunal finds a complaint of unfair dismissal is well founded the Tribunal has the power under s113 to exercise its discretion to make an order for reinstatement or re-engagement pursuant to s114 or s115. Under s116 in exercising its discretion whether to order reinstatement the Tribunal will consider firstly whether the claimant wishes to be reinstated and secondly whether it is practicable for the employer to comply with an order for reinstatement. S116(1)(c) provides that the tribunal shall consider, where the claimant has caused or contributed to the dismissal, whether it would be just to order reinstatement. However, in practice the circumstances in which an employee has been found to have contributed to an automatic unfair dismissal will be limited. If the Tribunal does not order reinstatement they will go on to consider re-engagement considering again the wishes of the employee, practicability and any issue of contribution.

If the claimant is not reinstated or re-engaged the Tribunal will award compensation consisting of a basic award and a compensatory award. The basic award will be calculated on the standard principles in s119 and a successful complaint under s99 is not one to which the minimum basic award provisions of s120 apply.

# CHAPTER EIGHT

# DISCRIMINATION

## Protection under the Equality Act 2010

### The Structure of the Act

Part 2, Chapter 1 of the Equality Act provides, in Section 4, a list of the nine specific characteristics which are protected under the Act which are collectively known as 'protected characteristics'. That list expressly includes 'pregnancy and maternity' as a distinct protected characteristic from 'sex'. Chapter 1 provides no further definition of 'pregnancy and maternity'.

Part 2, Chapter 2 of the Act sets out the prohibited conduct under the Act which is generally referred to as 'discrimination' and includes the familiar concepts of direct discrimination (s13), indirect discrimination (s19), harassment (s26) and victimisation (27) however it is important to be aware that 'pregnancy and maternity' is *not* a protected characteristic for all types of prohibited conduct within Chapter 2. Importantly, 'pregnancy and maternity' is *not* a protected characteristic for the purposes of indirect discrimination or harassment claims. The application of s13, direct discrimination is also qualified which is discussed in more detail below. The specific provisions for 'maternity and pregnancy' are contained in Section 18 of the Act. Section 18 is specifically concerned with 'pregnancy and maternity' *at work* (Section 17 deals with non-work cases which is beyond the scope of this book). As discussed in Chapter 4, following Brexit, the Government has produced the Retained EU Law (Revocation and Reform) Act 2023 ("REULA 23") in order to govern the amount and scope of law that is derived from EU Law. Importantly the effect of S2 of REULA is to repeal S4 of the European Withdrawal Act 2018, which retained EU

Law, from the end of 2023. In order to reproduce the effects of EU Equality law which would otherwise be repealed the Government has produced 'The Equality Act 2010 (Amendment) Regulations 2023' which amends the Equality Act from 1st January 2024. The effect of those amendments in relation to pregnancy and maternity is discussed below. The government has also produced an explanatory memorandum to the Regulations which provides a helpful explanation of what principles the amendments are intended to preserve.

From 1st January 2024 s18 Equality Act (with amendments in bold) provides:

> *S18 Pregnancy and maternity discrimination: work cases*
>
> *(1) This section has effect for the purposes of the application of Part 5 (work) to the protected characteristic of pregnancy and maternity.*
>
> *(2) A person (A) discriminates against a woman if, in* ***or after*** *the protected period in relation to a pregnancy of hers A treats her unfavourably-*
>
> > *(a) because of the pregnancy, or*
> >
> > *(b) because of illness suffered by her as a result of it.*
>
> *(3) A person (A) discriminates against a woman if A treats her unfavourably because she is on compulsory maternity leave* ***or on equivalent compulsory maternity leave****.*
>
> *(4) A person (A) discriminates against a woman if A treats her unfavourably because she is exercising or seeking to exercise, or has exercised or sought to exercise, the right to ordinary or additional maternity leave* ***or a right to equivalent maternity leave****.*
>
> *(5) For the purposes of subsection (2), if the treatment of a woman is in implementation of a decision taken in the protected period, the*

*treatment is to be regarded as occurring in that period (even if the implementation is not until after the end of that period).* ***[Repealed from 1st January 2024]***

*(6) The protected period, in relation to a woman's pregnancy, begins when the pregnancy begins, and ends-*

> *(a) if she has the right to ordinary and additional maternity leave, at the end of the additional maternity leave period or (if earlier) when she returns to work after the pregnancy;*
>
> ***(aa) if she does not have that right but has a right to equivalent maternity leave, at the end of that leave period, or (if earlier) when she returns to work after pregnancy:***
>
> *(b) if she does not have ~~that~~ a right* ***as described in paragraph (a) or (aa)****, at the end of the period of 2 weeks beginning with the end of the pregnancy.*

***(6A) For the purposes of this section-***

> ***"equivalent compulsory maternity leave" means a period of leave –***
>
> ***(a) Which is of a substantially similar nature (regardless of its length) to compulsory maternity leave, and***
>
> ***(b) Which is provided for under a statutory or contractual scheme;***

*(7) Section 13, so far as relating to sex discrimination, does not apply to treatment of a woman in so far as-*

> *(a) it is in* ***or after*** *the protected period in relation to her and is for a reason mentioned in paragraph (a) or (b) of subsection (2),*

*Or*

*(b) it is for a reason mentioned in subsection (3) or (4).*

'Work' is dealt with under Part 5, Chapter 1 of the Equality Act and by virtue of that part those protected by the prohibitions on discrimination include not only employees but also applicants (s39) and contract workers (s41). However, as will be seen some of the protections are in fact only afforded to those entitled to ordinary and additional maternity leave which is a right only afforded to employees.

Under s39 the following discrimination is prohibited in respect of applicants and employees:

- In the arrangements made for deciding to whom to offer employment
- As to the terms on which employment is offered
- Not offering employment.
- As to the terms of employment
- In the way the employer affords access, or does not afford access, to opportunities for promotion, transfer or training or for receiving any other benefit, facility or service
- By dismissing the employee
- By subjecting the employee to any other detriment.

Under s40 the following discrimination in prohibited against a contract worker;

- As to the terms on which the principle allows the worker to do the work

- By not allowing the worker to do, or to continue to do the work

- In the way the principle affords the worker access, or does not afford access, to opportunities for receiving a benefit, facility or service

The prohibition on discrimination due to pregnancy and maternity therefore falls into two broad categories. The first is unfavourable treatment due to pregnancy or illness due to pregnancy, this is a qualified protection limited to the 'protected period' and the second is a broader protection against unfavourable treatment due to maternity leave. In this Chapter we will consider the key elements of s18 that apply to both categories and also examine the specific limitations of the 'protected period'.

## EHRC Code of Practice

Guidance as to the interpretation and meaning of the Part 5 of the Equality Act is contained in the EHRC's Equality Act 2010 Statutory Code of Practice Employment. The Code may be used in evidence in legal proceedings brought under the Act and tribunals and courts must take into account any part of the Code which appears to be relevant to any questions arising in proceedings (para 1.13). Pregnancy and Maternity is dealt with in detail in Chapter Eight of the Code and contains practical examples of what treatment may amount to discrimination which can be a useful source for a practitioner.

## Background to statutory protection for Pregnancy and Maternity, no comparator needed

The protection from direct discrimination on the grounds of pregnancy and maternity derives from the Equal Treatment Directive. It was confirmed in *Dekker v. Stichting Vormingscentrum voor Jong Volwassenen (VJV-Centrum) Plus* [1992] ICR 325 and *Danmark A/S and Handels-og*

*Kontorfunktionaerernes Forbund I Danmark (HK) v. Dansk Arbejdsgiverforening* [1992] ICR 333 that discrimination against a woman on the ground of her pregnancy, and the absence from work which results, constituted direct discrimination contrary to the directive. The predecessor to the Equality Act, the Sex Discrimination Act 1975 did not originally make express provision for discrimination on the grounds of pregnancy however, in a series of appeals in the case of *Webb* culminating in *Webb v. Emo Air Cargo (UK) Ltd* [1995] ICR 1021 it was finally established that s1 SDA 75 could be construed as protecting women against discrimination on the grounds of pregnancy and, following a reference to the ECJ, that no comparator was required due to the unique state of pregnancy. The 1975 act was subsequently amended to expressly contain a prohibition on discrimination on the grounds of pregnancy (s3A(1)). In accordance with those principles s18 prohibits *unfavourable treatment* which is different to the language of s13, direct discrimination, which prohibits *less favourable treatment* and is a reflection of the fact that no comparator, actual or hypothetical, is needed for the purposes of s18.

## Unfavourable Treatment

The Act does not further define what is meant by unfavourable treatment. The EHRC Code of Practice makes reference to the types of prohibited conduct contained in s39 (para 8.21) but rather than provide further discussion as to the meaning of 'unfavourable treatment' it instead gives some examples of unfavourable treatment which will amount to discrimination (para 8.22). These are:

- failure to consult a woman on maternity leave about changes to her work or about possible redundancy
- disciplining a woman for refusing to carry out tasks due to pregnancy related risks

- assuming that a woman's work will become less important to her after childbirth and giving her less responsible or less interesting work as a result

- depriving a woman of her right to an annual assessment of her performance because she was on maternity leave;

- excluding a pregnant woman from business trips.

S15 EqA (discrimination arising from disability) also employs the term unfavourable treatment and the Code of Practice says in relation to s15 that to have been treated 'unfavourably' the individual must have been put at a disadvantage (para 5.7).

In most cases there is likely to be little dispute as to whether the alleged treatment would be 'unfavourable' and the threshold for unfavourable treatment is relatively low as was demonstrated in *Southwest Yorkshire Partnership NHS Foundation Trust v. Jackson and ors* UKEAT/0090/18/BA where the EAT found that a Tribunal had not erred in concluding that the act of the Respondent sending an email regarding redundancy to the Claimant's work email address when she was on maternity leave in circumstances where she learned of the email shortly afterwards and was not disadvantaged by the short delay was unfavourable treatment. However, an unjustified sense of grievance will not amount to 'unfavourable treatment' and it is not unfavourable treatment just because you could have been treated in a different *more* favourable way.

<u>'In relation to a pregnancy of hers'</u>

S18(2) requires that the unfavourable treatment is in relation to a pregnancy *of hers*. It is not, therefore, possible to make a claim under this provision if either the employer treated a woman unfavourably in the mistaken belief that she was pregnant or to bring a claim of discrimination by association. This is to be contrasted with s13 which prohibits less favourable treatment because of 'a protected characteristic' and does not expressly require the person complaining of less favourable treatment to have the specific characteristic themselves. Similarly s18(3) and (4) prohibit unfavourable treatment because a woman is exercising, has sought to exercise or exercised her right to maternity leave. The interaction between s13 and s18 is discussed further below.

'Because of'

Although s18 does not require a comparative exercise with an actual or hypothetical comparator it is not sufficient to point to the fact of pregnancy, related illness or maternity leave and the existence of unfavourable treatment to establish liability. The protected characteristic must be the *reason* for the unfavourable treatment. The question of causation in the context of maternity and pregnancy was considered in the pre-Equality Act case of *Johal v. Commission for Equality & Human Rights* UKEAT/0541/09/DA. The ET rejected a claim brought under s3A(1)(b) SDA 75 that Mrs Johal had been discriminated against by the EHRC when they had failed to inform her of an internal job opportunity whilst on maternity leave. The ET had found that the reason for the treatment was administrative error. The EAT rejecting Mrs Johal's appeal, considered the relevant case law on direct discrimination in general and in particular, the judgment of Underhill P (as he was at the time) in the case of *Amnesty International v. Ahmed* [2009] IRLR 884 where he reconciled the approaches taken in the earlier cases of *James v. Eastleigh Borough Council* and Lord Nicholls in *Nagarajan v. London Regional Transport* and the analysis of the Supreme Court in *R v. Jewish Free School Governing Body and others* [2009] IRLR 136. The EAT held (at para 23) that:

> *In simple terms, where an act is inherently discriminatory, for example, the difference in ages between men and women pensioners entitled to free swimming in Eastleigh Council's pools, the detriment suffered by the Claimant will be on the prohibited ground without*

> *more. The discriminator's motive for that discrimination, whether benign or malicious, is immaterial. However, where the act complained of is not in itself discriminatory, as we accept Ms Stone's submission applies in the present case, it may become so by discriminatory motivation, whether conscious or subconscious; the Nagarajan type of case.*
>
> *Thus, the critical question we think in the present case is the reason why question posed by Lord Nicholls: 'Why was the Claimant treated in the manner complained of?"*

The need to consider the reason for the treatment was emphasised in *Indigo Design Build and Management v. Martinez* UKEAT/0020/14/DM where it was particularly noted that the Tribunal had failed to apply the proper assessment in respect of s18 claims especially when contrasted with their correct approach in relation to allegations under s13. *Martinez* was applied by the EAT in the recent case of *Blackdown Hill Management Ltd and ors v. Tuchkova* EA-2021-000126-NT where the EAT upholding the Tribunal's finding of unfair dismissal due to redundancy found that it had failed to apply the correct causation test in respect of her s18 (and associated sex discrimination claims) or, if it had considered that the fact that the Claimant had exercised her right to maternity leave was more than a contextual or background matter, it had failed to explain why. It remains the case that when addressing Tribunals in s18 claims that do not require a comparator care needs to be taken to ensure they direct themselves correctly on causation.

It is not uncommon for claims to be brought under both the Equality Act and also under the ERA 96 and the associated Maternity and Paternity Regulations (which are considered in detail at Chapter 6) however, it is important to note that the need for the pregnancy or maternity to be the reason for the unfavourable treatment means that a breach of, for example, Regulation 10 MAPLE 99 (Redundancy during maternity leave), will not necessarily amount to discrimination. In *Sefton Borough Council v. Mrs M Wainwright* UKEAT/0168/14/LA it was argued that a breach of Regulation 10 must amount to inherent discrimination of the type identified in *Johal.* The EAT rejecting this argument held that while there may be many cases where the answer was the same the proposition that a breach of Regulation 10 meant there was inherent discrimination went beyond the language of the statute and held that the Tribunal had fallen into error in assuming the s18 question was answered by its finding that there had been a breach of the regulations.

## More than one reason for treatment?

As with s13 and s27, under s18 the discriminatory reason does not have to be the sole or even the principal reason for the treatment alleged. In *O'Neill v Governors of St Thomas More Roman Catholic Voluntary Aided Upper School* [1996] IRLR 372, EAT, the Claimant appealed a finding of the ET that she had not been discriminated against on the ground of her pregnancy pursuant to s1 SDA 75. The Tribunal had dismissed her claim on the basis that she had not been dismissed because of pregnancy *per se* but in circumstances where the Claimant, a religious education teacher, had become pregnant by a Roman Catholic Priest and this had come into the public domain. The EAT considered the appeal on the basis that the correct starting principle was that it was sufficient if pregnancy was *an* effective cause. They concluded that the Tribunal had fallen into error and that the term pregnancy *per se* was misleading because it suggested pregnancy as the sole ground for dismissal. They went on to state (at para 55):

> *Pregnancy always has surrounding circumstances, some arising prior to the state of pregnancy, some accompanying it, some consequential on it. The critical question is whether on an objective consideration of all the surrounding circumstances, the dismissal or other treatment complained of by the applicant is on the ground of pregnancy. It need not be only that ground. It need not even be mainly on that ground.*

The question of the extent to which the treatment had to be for the discriminatory reason was further considered by Lord Nicholls in the race discrimination and victimisation case of *Nagarajan.* He observed that decisions are frequently reached for more than one reason and that different words with 'different shades of meaning', including 'effective cause' had been used to reflect the application of the legislation in those circumstances. Noting that the application of legalistic phrases and subtle distinctions were best avoided he stated that *If racial grounds or protected acts had a significant influence on the outcome, discrimination is made out.*

## Knowledge of pregnancy

In order to establish discrimination under s18 the employer or principal will need to have known or correctly believed, or suspected, that the woman was pregnant, as the fact of the pregnancy (or its related illness) must be an operating cause in the mind of the alleged discriminator. As is discussed in Chapter 4, on entitlement to maternity leave there is no obligation for a woman to advise her employer of her pregnancy before the end of the fifteenth week before her expected week of childbirth however, if she has not informed her employer it may be difficult to prove that the employer had the requisite knowledge.

## Relevance of the decision maker

Identification of the decision maker(s) and their state of knowledge may be an important factor for a Claimant in establishing discrimination on the grounds of pregnancy and maternity. An example of the question of the state of knowledge of the imputed discriminator can be found in *Hair Division Ltd v. MacMillan* UKEATS/0033/12/BI. In that case the EAT found that the Tribunal had erred in imputing knowledge to the Managing Director of the Respondent company based on the fact that the Claimant's line manager who lived with the Managing Director and oversaw the day to day running of the business did have knowledge of the pregnancy. The EAT noted that the line manager was not the 'mind' of the company; there were no findings that she was a director and there were no findings to the effect that the line manager had informed the MD, who was rarely at the salon, that pregnancy had been confirmed.

A consideration of issues about decision-makers and reasons arose more recently in the EAT case of *Alcedo Orange Limited v. Ferridge-Gunn* EA-2022-000775-JOJ which concerned a woman who had been dismissed eight days after announcing she was pregnant. The Claimant complained about her dismissal relying, as background, on the comments and actions of her line manager who had provided information to the decision maker but did not make a separate complaint of discrimination in relation to those comments.

In giving judgment the EAT observed that to succeed in a claim of this type there must have been a discriminator or discriminators i.e. a person or persons who decided to dismiss the Claimant who were influenced by her pregnancy. They recognised that there were often challenges for a Claimant bringing a claim of this nature as she might not know who made the decision to dismiss, whether the decision was made by one person alone, whether that person might have been influenced by others or whether the decision was made jointly by a number of people. It was also highlighted that the identity of the decision maker(s) might become apparent from the pleadings, the case management or even during the hearing. Even in cases where the decision maker is never established it may be appropriate to draw an inference as to the motivation of the decision maker. The EAT gave guidance that an employment tribunal should, wherever, possible clearly set out who made the decision to dismiss and if there was more than once decision maker, what their roles were.

In the present case the Respondent appealed the decision of the Tribunal that they had directly discriminated against the Claimant by dismissing her arguing that the Tribunal had failed to separate the role of the decision maker from the manager who had provided information to him. In particular the Tribunal had failed to consider or apply the Court of Appeal decision of *Reynolds v. CLFIS (UK) Ltd* [2015] ICR 1010. *Reynolds* is authority for the fact that in a case which does not involve inherently discriminatory treatment or of joint decision making by more than one person acting with discriminatory motivation, only a person involved in the decision making who has a discriminatory motivation is liable. Therefore, where an innocent agent acts on 'tainted information' the discrimination is the supplying of the tainted information, not the acting upon it by its innocent recipient.

Importantly in this case, the represented Respondent had not raised *Reynolds* with the Tribunal which the EAT concluded they should have. This case contains some helpful discussion of the role of Tribunals in cases such as this where the Claimant was a litigant in person. If advising a Claimant on a claim of pregnancy discrimination, particularly in relation to dismissal consider:

- Can you identify the decision maker?

- Is this potentially a case of 'tainted information'? If so, consider including those matters as separate claims of unfavourable treatment.

- If you potentially have evidence of unfavourable treatment by way of 'tainted information' consider including those matters as discrete complaint of acts of discrimination in addition to any complaint of discriminatory dismissal.

- Review the information contained in the Response and any further information during case management, is an application to amend the claim needed?

- Do you have direct evidence of knowledge of pregnancy on the part of any identified decision maker? If not, is there evidence from which you can invite the Tribunal to conclude that they did have knowledge?

## Burden of Proof

The provisions of s136 EqA regarding the application of the burden of proof in proceedings under the EqA applies to s18 claims as it does to any proceedings relating to a contravention of the act.

The burden of proof provisions can prove useful to a Claimant in pregnancy cases. Although there is no requirement for a Claimant to prove less favourable treatment than an actual or hypothetical comparator, evidence of the treatment of others, or even the Claimant themselves before and after pregnancy can provide evidence which would allow the Tribunal to conclude that the burden of proof has shifted.

## The Protected Period

The prohibition on treating a woman unfavourably because of her pregnancy or because of an illness suffered because of it applies only during the 'protected period'. As can be seen the protected period is defined in s18(6) as beginning when the pregnancy begins and as ending:

- If she has the right to ordinary and additional maternity leave, at the end of the additional maternity leave, or if she returns earlier, when she returns to work after the pregnancy

- If she does not have the right to ordinary and additional maternity leave it ends at the end of 2 weeks beginning with the end of the pregnancy

The entitlement to ordinary and additional maternity leave is discussed in more detail in Chapter 4

## When does pregnancy begin?

The question of when pregnancy begins will normally not present much of an issue for a Tribunal especially as knowledge of the pregnancy will generally be required on the part of the employer. If an employee is undergoing IVF treatment she will be treated as pregnant from the date of implantation rather than the date of fertilisation of the ovum *in vitro, Mayr Backerei und Konditorei Geherd Flockner OHG* [2008] IRLR 387.

Discrimination in the context of IVF treatment is considered in more detail later in this chapter.

## The ending of the protected period

The protected period ends in the case of a woman who has been on ordinary or additional maternity leave when she returns to work after the pregnancy. In other circumstances it ends at the beginning of two weeks after the end of the pregnancy. One of the factors that weighed heavily in *Mayr* in determining that pregnancy did not begin until implantation rather than fertilisation of the ovum in vitro was that fertilised ova could be kept for many years during which implantation might remain contemplated meaning that there was no definitive point at which it could be said that pregnancy had come to an end.

It should be noted that the protected period will end when maternity leave ends even if the employee does not physically return to work due to for example, a period of sick absence (see *Lyons v. DWP Jobcentre Plus* [2014] ICR 668).

If the woman does not have a right to ordinary or additional maternity leave the protected period will end 2 weeks after the end of pregnancy. This situation will arise where the woman is not entitled to ordinary maternity leave, eg. she is a worker not an employee or where she suffers a miscarriage and does not qualify for maternity leave (a woman who otherwise qualifies and whose baby is stillborn after the 24th week of pregnancy is entitled to ordinary maternity leave).

## Unfavourable treatment outside the protected period

S18(5) provided that if the unfavourable treatment was the implementation of a decision the relevant question was when the decision was made. If the decision was made during the protected period s18 would apply even if the implementation of the decision occurred after the end of a protected period. On the face of it s18 did not cover the situation where a decision was made outside the protected period but related to something that occurred within the protected period. However, in the case of *Brown v. Rentokil* [1998] ICR 790, the European Court of Justice considered the position of a pregnant woman who developed pregnancy related illness in the early stages of her pregnancy and was dismissed before the birth of her child on the basis of a contractual clause. In holding that this was unlawful the Court considered the wider law in relation to dismissals for absences relating to pregnancy-related illness. Importantly they disapproved of the Court's dicta in *Handels- og Kontorfunktionoerernes Forbund I Danmark v. Dansk Handel and Service* [1997] ECR I-2757 (also referred to as "*Larsson")* stating that, contrary to the court's ruling in that case:

> *Where a woman is absent owing to illness resulting from pregnancy or childbirth, and that illness arose during pregnancy and persisted during and after maternity leave, her absence not only during maternity leave but also during the period extending from the start of her pregnancy to the start of her maternity cannot be taken into account for computation of the period justifying her dismissal under*

*national law. As to her absence after maternity leave, that may be taken into account under the same conditions as a man's absence, of the same duration, through incapacity for work* (para 27).

In order to give effect to this principle following the repeal of s4 of the European Withdrawal Act 2018, from the 1st January 2024 the Equality Act amendment regulations amend s18(2) to include unfavourable treatment 'in *or after*' the protected period which is because of her pregnancy or because of an illness suffered by her as a result of it. S18(5) is repealed.

Pregnancy related illness?

What amounts to a 'pregnancy related illness' is not defined in the act or the Code of Practice. The Code does provide at Para 8.22

*As examples only, it will amount to pregnancy and maternity discrimination to treat a woman unfavourably during the protected period for the following reasons:*

- *The fact that, because of her pregnancy, the woman will be temporarily unable to do the job for which she is specifically employed whether permanently or on a fixed-term contract*
- *The pregnant woman is temporarily unable to work because to do so would be breach of health and safety regulations*
- *The costs to the business of covering her work*
- *Any absence due to pregnancy related illness*
- *Her inability to attend a disciplinary hearing due to morning sickness or other pregnancy-related conditions;*

- *Performance issues due to morning sickness or other pregnancy-related conditions*

In many cases there may be no dispute that the illness is pregnancy related but if there is any doubt women would be well advised to ask their GP to provide a fit note confirming that the condition is pregnancy related.

Interplay between S18 and Sex discrimination

S18(7) expressly provides that s13, direct discrimination, does not apply, as far as it relates to *sex*, in relation to the treatment of a woman if the complaint is about unfavourable treatment:

- Because of pregnancy or because of illness suffered by her as a result of it *and* it is in (or after) the protected period *or*
- Because she is on compulsory maternity leave
- Because she is exercising or seeking to exercise, or has exercised or sought to exercise, the right to ordinary or additional maternity leave

On the face of it, a claim relating to detriment because of pregnancy or pregnancy related illness within the protected period or maternity leave will *not* form the basis of a claim of sex discrimination however s13 does not otherwise limit its application to pregnancy and maternity.

S13(6)(a) expressly deals with breastfeeding, providing that unfavourable treatment on the grounds of sex includes less favourable treatment of a woman because she is breastfeeding. Although s13(7) disapplied this provision for Part V (work) the case of *Otero Ramos v. Servicio Galego de Saude and another* [2018] ICR 965 confirmed that that less favourable treatment of a worker due to her being a breastfeeding mother would be direct discrimination on the grounds of sex. Accordingly, s13(7) has been removed by the 2023 Amendment Regulations. When advising a Claimant it is important to consider:

- If the complaint is about treatment due to pregnancy or pregnancy related illness was the unfavourable treatment in relation to matters which occurred in the protected period? If there is any doubt the claim should be put as a s13 claim in the alternative

- Is the complaint about indirect discrimination or harassment? If so there is no protection for the protected characteristic of pregnancy and maternity and therefore consideration should be given as to whether it is due to the protected characteristic of sex

- Has there been unfavourable treatment because of a mistaken belief that the Claimant was pregnant? If so is there potentially a direct discrimination claim on the grounds of sex

- Is the complaint of discrimination by association, in which case consider whether it might be sex discrimination

As we have seen there is no need for an actual or hypothetical comparator for the purposes of s18 as the question is whether the woman has been treated unfavourably because of her protected characteristic. The wording of s13 is of less favourable treatment and usually requires an actual or hypothetical comparator who satisfies the conditions of s23 EqA. In the case of *The Commissioner of the City of London Police v. Geldhart* [2021] ICR 1329 the question arose as to whether a comparator was needed in a claim of direct sex discrimination brought under s13 in relation to pregnancy and maternity. On the facts of that case the Claimant could not rely on s18 in respect of a claim for failure to pay a 'London Allowance' for the duration of her maternity leave and therefore brought a claim of direct sex discrimination under s13. The EAT rejected the contention that the introduction of s3(A) in the SDA 1975 (and by extension s18 EqA) had rendered *Webb v. EMO Cargo* redundant and agreed with the ET that no comparator was needed under s13 when the claim was in relation to pregnancy and maternity. The Court of Appeal partially allowed the Commissioner's appeal holding that the reason for the Claimant's treatment was 'absence' rather than 'maternity absence'. As a result of their conclusions they did not have to expressly decide the question of the argument that *Webb* had been rendered redundant but Underhill LJ noted that he was not surprised that the ET and EAT had found the argument unconvincing. This issue has also been addressed by the Amendment Regulations by amending s18(3), (4) (6)(aa) to include 'a right to equivalent maternity leave' in addition to ordinary or additional maternity leave. 'Equivalent compulsory maternity leave' is now defined in a new s18(6)(A).

S13(6)(b) also provides that if the protected characteristic is sex that in a case where B is a man, no account is to be taken of the special treatment afforded to a woman in connection with pregnancy or childbirth. This section has also been amended by virtue of the Amendment Regulations to add 'maternity'.

## IVF Treatment

As discussed above a woman undergoing IVF will be pregnant for the purposes of S18 from the date of implantation. However, the question arises as to what protections an employee who is undergoing IVF treatment may have under the Equality Act given its close connection to pregnancy and maternity.

In the case of *London Borough of Greenwich v. Robinson* EAT/745/94 an employer used sickness absence, excluding pregnancy related absences, as a selection criteria for a redundancy exercise. The Claimant's sick record included 29 days absence for IVF treatment. The EAT allowed the employers appeal against a finding that she had been discriminated against on the grounds of her sex within the meaning of s1 SDA 75 finding that infertility was a medical condition requiring treatment and should be treated as sickness in the usual way.

In the ECJ case of *Mayr Backerei und Konditorei Geherd Flockner OHG* [2008] IRLR 387 an employee underwent follicular puncture with a view to implantation five days later, during which time she was certified sick. In the period between follicular puncture and implantation the employee was dismissed. The ECJ whilst accepting that she could not be said to be pregnant and afford herself of the specific protections of Council Directive 02/85/EEC (the Pregnancy Directive) which had come into force in 2004 until implantation had occurred, held that she was entitled to protection under the Equal Treatment Directive. They held that:

> *It is true that workers of both sexes can be temporarily prevented from carrying out their work on account of medical treatment they must receive. Nevertheless, the treatment in question in the main proceedings – namely a follicular puncture and the transfer to the woman's uterus of the ova removed by way of that follicular puncture immediately after their fertilisation – directly affects only women. It follows that the dismissal of a female worker essentially because she is undergoing that important stage of in vitro fertilisation treatment constitutes direct discrimination on the grounds of sex.*

The impact of the decision in *Mayr* on *Robinson* was considered in *Sahota v. The Home Office & Pipkin* UKEAT/0342/09/LA. The appeal was ultimately decided on different grounds but the EAT considered it right to express a view on the issue as it might be of relevance in other cases. On behalf of the Claimant it was contended that *Robinson* was inconsistent with *Mayr.* On behalf of the employer it was accepted that *Robinson* required some modification in light of *Mayr* but that *Mayr* was not authority for the proposition that any less favourable treatment of a woman on the ground she was receiving IVF treatment constituted sex discrimination. The EAT whilst accepting that there was a reasonable argument that *Mayr* was intended to extend wider than the narrow facts of that particular case on the basis that IVF treatment as a whole only directly affects women ultimately expressed the view that the wider argument was 'too much'. To accept this would encompass any kind of gender-specific treatment a proposition which has been rejected in the original ECJ rulings in *Dekker.* They therefore concluded that the Court in *Mayr* was *evidently willing to make a limited, and closely defined, exception only for the 'important' stage "between follicular puncture and the immediate transfer of the in vitro fertilised ova."*

Therefore the fact that a woman is undergoing IVF treatment is unlikely to give her protection under the Equality Act in relation to treatment related absence except in a specific narrowly defined window of time.

## Complaints to the Employment Tribunal

The requirement for ACAS early conciliation applies to a complaint of discrimination under the EqA 10. Pursuant to s123 the time limit for bringing a complaint is three months starting with the date of the act to which the complaint relates. That time limit will be modified by any extension to take account of early conciliation. Often a Claimant will complain of a series of acts and allege that it was conduct extending over a period. Pursuant to s123(3) in such circumstances the act will be treated as having been done at the end of that period. Further pursuant to s123(1)(b) the Tribunal has a discretion to consider a claim presented within such further period as it considers it just and equitable to do so. Unless it is apparent that the entirety of the Claim has been presented outside the three-month period a Tribunal will usually defer questions as to continuing act and any just and equitable extension until the final hearing.

The remedies open to the Tribunal are contained in s124 and include:

- A declaration as to the rights of the complainant.

- An award of compensation

- Recommendations

An award of compensation will usually include an award for injury to feelings applying the principles contained in *Vento v. Chief Constable of West Yorkshire* [2003] IRLR 102. Following *De Souza v. Vinci Construction (UK) Ltd* [2017] EWCA Civ 879 the guidelines have been subject to annual increases contained in Presidential Guidance. The relevant rates are determined by reference to the date of presentation of the claim to the Tribunal. For claims presented on after the 6$^{th}$ April 2023 the relevant bands are:

- Lower Band £1,100 – £11,200 (less serious cases)

- Middle Band £11,200 – £33,700 (cases that do not merit an award in the upper band)

- Upper Band £33,700 – £56,200 (the most serious cases). The most exceptional cases may exceed £56,200

In *Vento* the Court of Appeal cited with approval the dicta in *Prison Service and ors v. Johnson* [1997] ICR 275 EAT which provided a summary of the principles in relation to injury to feelings including:

- Awards for ITF are compensatory and must be just to both parties. They should provide full compensation without punishing the discriminator. Accordingly, such awards should not be increased due to feelings of indignation at the guilty party's conduct.

- Awards shouldn't be so low so as to diminish respect of the policy of the legislation. Society has condemned discrimination and awards ensure it is seen to be wrong. Conversely, awards should not be so excessive that they might be regarded as untaxed riches.

- Awards should be broadly similar to the range of awards in personal injury cases.
- Tribunals should bear in mind the value in everyday life of the sum they are contemplating this can be done by reference to purchasing power or by reference to earnings.
- Tribunals should have regard to the fact that there is a need for the public to have respect for the levels of award made.

The level of award will depend on the facts of the particular case but it is not uncommon for Tribunal to be mindful of the impact of discrimination on a woman at what should be a happy time and discriminatory dismissals may well fall to be awarded at least in the middle band.

# MORE BOOKS BY LAW BRIEF PUBLISHING

A selection of our other titles available now:-

| |
|---|
| 'A Practical Guide to the Independent School Standards – September 2023 Edition' by Sarah McKimm |
| 'A Practical Guide to Estate Administration and Crypto Assets' by Richard Marshall |
| 'A Practical Guide to Managing GDPR Data Subject Access Requests – Second Edition' by Patrick O'Kane |
| 'A Practical Guide to Parental Alienation in Private and Public Law Children Cases' by Sam King QC & Frankie Shama |
| 'Contested Heritage – Removing Art from Land and Historic Buildings' by Richard Harwood QC, Catherine Dobson, David Sawtell |
| 'The Limits of Separate Legal Personality: When Those Running a Company Can Be Held Personally Liable for Losses Caused to Third Parties Outside of the Company' by Dr Mike Wilkinson |
| 'A Practical Guide to Transgender Law' by Robin Moira White & Nicola Newbegin |
| 'A Practical Guide to 'Stranded Spouses' in Family Law' by Mani Singh Basi |
| 'A Practical Guide to Residential Freehold Conveyancing' by Lorraine Richardson |
| 'A Practical Guide to Pensions on Divorce for Lawyers' by Bryan Scant |
| 'A Practical Guide to Challenging Sham Marriage Allegations in Immigration Law' by Priya Solanki |
| 'A Practical Guide to Digital Communications Evidence in Criminal Law' by Sam Willis |
| 'A Practical Guide to Legal Rights in Scotland' by Sarah-Jane Macdonald |
| 'A Practical Guide to New Build Conveyancing' by Paul Sams & Rebecca East |
| 'A Practical Guide to Defending Barristers in Disciplinary Cases' by Marc Beaumont |
| 'A Practical Guide to Inherited Wealth on Divorce' by Hayley Trim |
| 'A Practical Guide to Practice Direction 12J and Domestic Abuse in Private Law Children Proceedings' by Rebecca Cross & Malvika Jaganmohan |

| |
|---|
| 'A Practical Guide to Confiscation and Restraint'<br>by Narita Bahra QC, John Carl Townsend, David Winch |
| 'A Practical Guide to the Law of Forests in Scotland' by Philip Buchan |
| 'A Practical Guide to Health and Medical Cases in Immigration Law'<br>by Rebecca Chapman & Miranda Butler |
| 'A Practical Guide to Bad Character Evidence for Criminal Practitioners<br>by Aparna Rao |
| 'A Practical Guide to Extradition Law post-Brexit' by Myles Grandison et al |
| 'A Practical Guide to Hoarding and Mental Health for Housing Lawyers'<br>by Rachel Coyle |
| 'A Practical Guide to Psychiatric Claims in Personal Injury – 2nd Edition'<br>by Liam Ryan |
| 'Stephens on Contractual Indemnities' by Richard Stephens |
| 'A Practical Guide to the EU Succession Regulation' by Richard Frimston |
| 'A Practical Guide to Solicitor and Client Costs – 2nd Edition' by Robin Dunne |
| 'Constructive Dismissal – Practice Pointers and Principles' by Benjimin Burgher |
| 'A Practical Guide to Religion and Belief Discrimination Claims in the Workplace'<br>by Kashif Ali |
| 'A Practical Guide to the Law of Medical Treatment Decisions' by Ben Troke |
| 'Fundamental Dishonesty and QOCS in Personal Injury Proceedings: Law and Practice' by Jake Rowley |
| 'A Practical Guide to the Law in Relation to School Exclusions'<br>by Charlotte Hadfield & Alice de Coverley |
| 'A Practical Guide to Divorce for the Silver Separators' by Karin Walker |
| 'The Right to be Forgotten – The Law and Practical Issues' by Melissa Stock |
| 'A Practical Guide to Planning Law and Rights of Way in National Parks, the Broads and AONBs' by James Maurici QC, James Neill et al |
| 'A Practical Guide to Election Law' by Tom Tabori |
| 'A Practical Guide to the Law in Relation to Surrogacy' by Andrew Powell |
| 'A Practical Guide to Claims Arising from Fatal Accidents – 2nd Edition'<br>by James Patience |
| 'A Practical Guide to the Ownership of Employee Inventions – From Entitlement to Compensation' by James Tumbridge & Ashley Roughton |
| 'A Practical Guide to Asbestos Claims' by Jonathan Owen & Gareth McAloon |

'A Practical Guide to Stamp Duty Land Tax in England and Northern Ireland' by Suzanne O'Hara

'A Practical Guide to the Law of Farming Partnerships' by Philip Whitcomb

'Covid-19, Homeworking and the Law – The Essential Guide to Employment and GDPR Issues' by Forbes Solicitors

'Covid-19 and Criminal Law – The Essential Guide' by Ramya Nagesh

'Covid-19 and Family Law in England and Wales – The Essential Guide' by Safda Mahmood

'A Practical Guide to the Law of Unlawful Eviction and Harassment – 2nd Edition' by Stephanie Lovegrove

'Covid-19, Brexit and the Law of Commercial Leases – The Essential Guide' by Mark Shelton

'A Practical Guide to Costs in Personal Injury Claims – 2nd Edition' by Matthew Hoe

'A Practical Guide to the General Data Protection Regulation (GDPR) – 2nd Edition' by Keith Markham

'Ellis on Credit Hire – Sixth Edition' by Aidan Ellis & Tim Kevan

'A Practical Guide to Working with Litigants in Person and McKenzie Friends in Family Cases' by Stuart Barlow

'Protecting Unregistered Brands: A Practical Guide to the Law of Passing Off' by Lorna Brazell

'A Practical Guide to Secondary Liability and Joint Enterprise Post-Jogee' by Joanne Cecil & James Mehigan

'A Practical Guide to the Pre-Action RTA Claims Protocol for Personal Injury Lawyers' by Antonia Ford

'A Practical Guide to Neighbour Disputes and the Law' by Alexander Walsh

'A Practical Guide to Forfeiture of Leases' by Mark Shelton

'A Practical Guide to Coercive Control for Legal Practitioners and Victims' by Rachel Horman

'A Practical Guide to the Law of Driverless Cars – Second Edition' by Alex Glassbrook, Emma Northey & Scarlett Milligan

'A Practical Guide to TOLATA Claims' by Greg Williams

'A Practical Guide to Elderly Law – 2nd Edition' by Justin Patten

'A Practical Guide to Responding to Housing Disrepair and Unfitness Claims' by Iain Wightwick

| |
|---|
| 'A Practical Guide to the Law of Bullying and Harassment in the Workplace' by Philip Hyland |
| 'How to Be a Freelance Solicitor: A Practical Guide to the SRA-Regulated Freelance Solicitor Model' by Paul Bennett |
| 'A Practical Guide to Prison Injury Claims' by Malcolm Johnson |
| 'A Practical Guide to the Small Claims Track – 2nd Edition' by Dominic Bright |
| 'A Practical Guide to Advising Clients at the Police Station' by Colin Stephen McKeown-Beaumont |
| 'A Practical Guide to Antisocial Behaviour Injunctions' by Iain Wightwick |
| 'Practical Mediation: A Guide for Mediators, Advocates, Advisers, Lawyers, and Students in Civil, Commercial, Business, Property, Workplace, and Employment Cases' by Jonathan Dingle with John Sephton |
| 'The Mini-Pupillage Workbook' by David Boyle |
| 'A Practical Guide to Crofting Law' by Brian Inkster |
| 'A Practical Guide to the Law of Domain Names and Cybersquatting' by Andrew Clemson |
| 'A Practical Guide to the Law of Gender Pay Gap Reporting' by Harini Iyengar |
| 'NHS Whistleblowing and the Law' by Joseph England |
| 'Employment Law and the Gig Economy' by Nigel Mackay & Annie Powell |
| 'A Practical Guide to Noise Induced Hearing Loss (NIHL) Claims' by Andrew Mckie, Ian Skeate, Gareth McAloon |
| 'An Introduction to Beauty Negligence Claims – A Practical Guide for the Personal Injury Practitioner' by Greg Almond |
| 'Intercompany Agreements for Transfer Pricing Compliance' by Paul Sutton |
| 'Zen and the Art of Mediation' by Martin Plowman |
| 'A Practical Guide to the SRA Principles, Individual and Law Firm Codes of Conduct 2019 – What Every Law Firm Needs to Know' by Paul Bennett |
| 'A Practical Guide to Adoption for Family Lawyers' by Graham Pegg |
| 'A Practical Guide to Industrial Disease Claims' by Andrew Mckie & Ian Skeate |
| 'A Practical Guide to Conducting a Sheriff Court Proof' by Andrew Stevenson |
| 'A Practical Guide to Vicarious Liability' by Mariel Irvine |
| 'A Practical Guide to Applications for Landlord's Consent and Variation of Leases' by Mark Shelton |
| 'A Practical Guide to Relief from Sanctions Post-Mitchell and Denton' by Peter Causton |

| |
|---|
| 'A Practical Guide to Equity Release for Advisors' by Paul Sams |
| 'A Practical Guide to Financial Services Claims' by Chris Hegarty |
| 'The Law of Houses in Multiple Occupation: A Practical Guide to HMO Proceedings' by Julian Hunt |
| 'Occupiers, Highways and Defective Premises Claims: A Practical Guide Post-Jackson – 2nd Edition' by Andrew Mckie |
| 'A Practical Guide to Financial Ombudsman Service Claims' by Adam Temple & Robert Scrivenor |
| 'A Practical Guide to Running Housing Disrepair and Cavity Wall Claims: 2nd Edition' by Andrew Mckie & Ian Skeate |
| 'A Practical Guide to Holiday Sickness Claims – 2nd Edition' by Andrew Mckie & Ian Skeate |
| 'Arguments and Tactics for Personal Injury and Clinical Negligence Claims' by Dorian Williams |
| 'A Practical Guide to Drone Law' by Rufus Ballaster, Andrew Firman, Eleanor Clot |
| 'A Practical Guide to Compliance for Personal Injury Firms Working With Claims Management Companies' by Paul Bennett |
| 'RTA Allegations of Fraud in a Post-Jackson Era: The Handbook – 2nd Edition' by Andrew Mckie |
| 'RTA Personal Injury Claims: A Practical Guide Post-Jackson' by Andrew Mckie |
| 'On Experts: CPR35 for Lawyers and Experts' by David Boyle |
| 'An Introduction to Personal Injury Law' by David Boyle |

These books and more are available to order online direct from the publisher at www.lawbriefpublishing.com, where you can also read free sample chapters. For any queries, contact us on 0844 587 2383 or mail@lawbriefpublishing.com.

Our books are also usually in stock at www.amazon.co.uk with free next day delivery for Prime members, and at good legal bookshops such as Wildy & Sons.

We are regularly launching new books in our series of practical day-to-day practitioners' guides. Visit our website and join our free newsletter to be kept informed and to receive special offers, free chapters, etc.

You can also follow us on Twitter at www.twitter.com/lawbriefpub.

www.ingramcontent.com/pod-product-compliance
Lightning Source LLC
LaVergne TN
LVHW022113200926
848481LV00003B/1165
*9781914608988*